OFF THE GRID
WITHOUT A PADDLE

Lynne Farr

LULU.COM

Cover design by Patti Millington
Back cover photo: Carlini Nunez

ISBN: 978-1-4357-1571-4

Library of Congress Control Number: 2008903997

Printed in the United States of America.

Preface

OFF THE GRID WITHOUT A PADDLE is the true story of two greenhorns, escapees from the gritty City Of Los Angeles, who buy a home off the grid in a tropical mountain rainforest in rural Hawaii, with fantasies of utopia and dreams of self-sufficiency, but no real idea of what they're getting into.

In their first year in an unfamiliar new world, the high-tech, low-tech, no-tech learning curve is steep and hilarious: exasperating, exhilarating . . . exciting!

OFF THE GRID WITHOUT A PADDLE answers the questions:

Why is a former Hollywood television producer standing in the middle of a single track road in a Hawaiian jungle in the pouring rain juggling a cell phone and an umbrella as she tries to make a phone call to her bank?

Can an internationally known fine-artist and self-professed "city boy" cut down dead trees with a chainsaw and split logs with a long-handled axe?

Who installed the solar panels backwards?

Why is the water pump making that burping noise?

Are wild pigs really dangerous?

Why would anyone bake their clothes?

For the answers to these and other important questions of survival, read on . . .

Contents

CONTENTS Continued

"The most successful people are those who are good at Plan B."

\- James York

1

PARADISE WANTED
From A Concrete Jungle To A Real One

We bought our beautiful home on The Big Island of Hawaii from a man who didn't really want to sell it. He told us, my husband and I, that he'd built the place to suit his own simple lifestyle and had planned to spend the rest of his life living there on his fern-tree and flower filled half-acre of Eden.

He said he didn't much like people, which is why he'd chosen to build far away from them at the very end of an almost uninhabited country lane, half a mile from the nearest paved road, in a mountain rainforest, off the electric grid, with no city water, no sewer system, no phone line, no TV reception, no street address, no postal delivery, no garbage pickup, and no road maintenance.

He said the reason the house was for sale was that he'd gotten married. His wife had young grandchildren in Florida whom she missed too much, so she'd arm-twisted him into moving to Sarasota.

He seemed so unnerved by this big-city commitment - the people thing - and the impending loss of his uniquely lovely habitat, the hand-built home and the stunning gardens in which he'd invested so much time and talent, that I boldly said to him, "Maybe you should divorce the woman and keep the house." "We talked about it," he said.

We couldn't say the house was perfect for us: we'd never lived in one. Moving to a house would be a complete departure from anything we'd known in our fifteen years together, most of which we'd spent in a rented live/work studio loft of 2,500 square feet, with twelve foot ceilings, factory skylights, French windows, brick walls, and high-gloss bird's-eye maple floors, on the second floor of a ninety-year-old former ink warehouse in downtown Los Angeles.

Life there was an ongoing party with our non-conformist neighbors who were mostly artists, like my husband, writers like me, photographers, film-makers, musicians, or struggling entrepreneurs, all of us trying to give form to our brilliant, or farfetched, ideas in a depressed, therefore cheap, industrial neighborhood overdue for urban renewal.

We'd partied through the earthquake retrofit of the First Street Bridge, which abutted our lofts, with jackhammers going off from 6:00 in the morning and cement dust sifting onto every horizontal surface.

We'd partied through the building and start-up of the car-wash for the Metropolitan Transportation Authority's new subway line, located directly below our bedroom windows: the constant construction, the noisy pumps, the screeching train wheels on wet-then-rusty tracks, the honking of every train that passed through the car-wash at any hour, day or night.

We'd partied through the bang-bang, shoot-shoot of movie companies filming bloody crime sagas on our graffiti'd streets; the roar of police helicopters with searchlights and bullhorns chasing down the real-life criminals; the smell of "pork night" when a nearby slaughter-house infused our lofts with the nauseating perfume of over-ripe dead pigs.

Speaking of pigs: Right now there's a crowd of the local wild ones rooting around in the woods beside our house.

I've never heard anything like the sounds they're making, "Ack ack ack, snuffle snuffle snuffle, ACK ACK ACK, snort snort," as loud as a motorcycle without a muffler. But I'm sure it's pigs. I can hear the babies squealing.

I'm looking out the door and I can hear them coming closer.
And closer . . .

I can't see them, but, trust me, I won't be tiptoeing into the bushes to spy on them any time soon because I'm terrified. Fern fronds are flapping. Branches are snapping. Whoever is out there is LARGE!

In L. A., we'd huddled with our neighbors through the dripping heat of summer and the chill of winter in our uninsulated building. We'd smiled, bravely, at an influx of stereo sub-woofers and DJ's-in-training who thumped up the night. We'd planted trees and flowers on barren streets and rescued baby pigeons. We'd rescued each other when trouble came. It was an intense, never dull way to live, but we believed, we hoped, not for everyone.

Then, gradually and perhaps inevitably, L. A.'s "Downtown" became trendy; with appropriate irony, right around the time The City put up signs designating our neighborhood as "The Artists' District."

Real estate values went up. So did rents in our building, sky high. And as they rose, our tightly knit community of artists moved: one to India, one to Spain, one to New York, two to Paris, two to Arizona, two to Turkey; the rest of us scattered around the city.

"ACK, snort, ROOT, rustle, GRUNT," those pigs can't be more than thirty feet away. I feel like locking all the doors, but . . . thinking it through, that's probably not necessary. Pigs can't turn a doorknob in the first place. And they don't come into people's houses. Do they???

Of course, we knew there'd be wild pigs on Hawaii Island. The seller of our house had told us he'd seen them nearby. Did he hunt them? Not since he found God, but he used to.

In any case, they were here long before we were. They're an integral part of Hawaiian culture: what's a luau without a pig? The earliest Hawaiians brought them here from Polynesia in their double-hulled canoes to raise for food. I'd even read that in primitive times women used to fatten baby pigs on breast milk. But then I looked them up on the internet: "The Feral Pig (Sus Scrofa)," and saw the size of a full grown boar. They can grow to 450 kilograms. That would be 992 pounds. That's half a ton. Yikes! And they have these nasty tusks. And, like the man who built this house, they're not that fond of people.

I had owned a home on the Hawaiian island of Kauai the whole time we lived in Downtown. I'd bought it planning to move there permanently after opting out of the daily grind, the depressing politics, the ego-tripping, the no-fun-anymore, of being a staff television comedy writer/producer in Hollywood.

Looking back, I can say I was probably spoiled and too young to appreciate a job other people would kill for: when you have curly hair you wish it was straight. But after working on a couple of long running hits, *The Bob Newhart Show* and *The Love Boat*, I co-created a series, with too much lowest-common-denominator input from too many Network Vice-Presidents Of Development, which was roundly panned by the critics, and all too rapidly cancelled.

We Got It Made was described by one member of the press as "the wart on NBC's schedule," and Grant Tinker, head of the network, said publicly, "It's not a show I would watch." I still wonder if the CEO of Kraft Foods would tell reporters, "Cheez Whiz? I wouldn't eat it."

I found out the series was cancelled by reading it in *The Hollywood Reporter*. No phone call? No personal note from people I'd been working with for over two years? How cold is that?

In "there-must-be-more-to-life-than-this" mode, I said goodbye to network television and aimed myself in a new direction, one in which there was time to breath, time for reflection, time to learn, time for friends, and time to write, hopefully, a non-wart.

Buying a little house on Kauai was the symbol of my new priorities, but, as things worked out, I never even spent a night in it.

How come? Blame it on love. I met the man who would become my other half, and moving there was not an option for him.

What is it about love? Is it biology, or chemistry, or psychology that can make you jettison schemes you've fervently schemed? Is it weird science, or just that the person who walks into your life looks a

4

little like your favorite uncle, or doesn't look anything like Grant Tinker, or is smart, or deep, or talented, or is kind to old people, or likes cats, or doesn't drink, or does smoke, or makes you laugh?

I don't know the answer, though I don't think you choose love. I think it chooses you. It points its foxy finger and holds out its trickster hand. If you refuse it, you might be missing something.

I did a one-eighty over a man named Shingo Honda, a fine artist from Japan, who's taller than my favorite uncle and has much better posture, who does like cats (not that I do), who is very kind to old people, and who really makes me laugh.

And not just because of his Japanese way with the English language, in which "first" becomes "fast," and "fast" becomes "first"; "pilot" becomes "pirate" or "parrot"; a fork is a "hork" and a horse is a "force"; and "birth," "bus," "bath," "boss," and "bass," are indistinguishable from one another.

I shelved my plans to move to Hawaii and instead moved, with him, into the bowels of Los Angeles.

He's a painter, printmaker, and installation artist with an international reputation, who likes to work big. Aside from wanting to be in L. A. where the art action was, he and my tiny house on Kauai were as wrong for each other as we were right.

I made the hard decision to rent the house out and only made one trip there to fix it up between tenants.

Fortunately for us, fifteen years later, as land values rose in Los Angeles, they boomed on Kauai, and I was able to sell the property and put some decent money in the bank.

That money couldn't translate into a home of our own in, or even near, L. A. though. Prices there were too rich for our blood, and we, two free-lancers, weren't all that mortgage-worthy.

Who wanted a mortgage anyway? Who wanted to live in The City Of The Angels any more, with half our friends gone, and daily warnings of looming terrorism overshadowing nightly reports of drive-by shootings?

I dusted off my dream of living in the incomparable Hawaiian Islands, with their temperate weather, gorgeous views, and laid-back lifestyle.

I'd heard that The Big Island, Hawaii, was the last place where property was still affordable: people were selling their high priced homes on the U. S. mainland and on other islands and moving over.

Shingo (say it like Ringo) had an art show coming up in Thailand, so we booked a triangle ticket that would let us stop in Hawaii on our way back to L. A. to have a look for ourselves. We'd visit friends and friends of friends who lived on The Big Island and ask them how they liked it. With no commitment, though: we were "just looking."

After exploring Hawaii Island for a week, we could say that we liked the rainy, eastern, Hilo side best. It was less developed and less touristy than the sunny west side Kona Coast, with its huge resorts and malls, its condo sprawl and traffic, and its chain-store state of mind.

Mainly agricultural, East Hawaii was still unspoiled. Places named as towns were little more than crossroads, with a general store, a gas station, a post office, and some wooden houses painted in pastel colors making a community.

Open fields, and bamboo forests, and ancient cemeteries going to seed beside the highway, and rusting ghost equipment from bygone sugar days, were framed by views of the glittering Pacific Ocean and the mountains, Mauna Kea and Mauna Loa, draped in their dramatic cloud finery. Trees with trunks twelve feet around, vines that climbed to dizzy heights and bloomed, mile after mile of fragrantly perfumed flowers: yeah!

In Hilo, East Hawaii's only real town, Hawaiian names identified the streets and landmarks, buildings wore as many Asian names as English, and Buddhist temples were as prominent as churches. Though it had its fast food, big box stores, and supermarkets, they hadn't crowded out the farmers' market with its stalls of locally grown fresh everything. Nearby, there were both upscale and hole-in-the-wall places to eat international food.

6

And East Hawaii still had genuine aloha, people who were friendly and open, who'd laugh at the drop of a hat. Their smiles were instant and real and they lit up our every day. And I'm talking about strangers. Our friends and their friends added fun and advice. The sum total? Nothing negative.

But though we felt at home in East Hawaii, we hadn't, by any means, decided to make it our home. In fact, Shingo, whose English we call "Shinglish," kept saying, "Why I need move Hawaii? I am city boy."

Wow! Oh, Wow! An entire pig family is coming out of the woods and crossing under my window.

They're not so big. The Mom is black and white, the size of a barnyard pig, and she has one, two, three, four, EIGHT little babies. Four are pure black, and four are multi-colored in shades of brown and white and dusty pink. They're as stocky and sculptural as though they'd been chipped out of granite.

Dozy, adorably bumping into each other, Mom is herding them across our lawn. Now they're crossing the road, and ambling through the wild bamboo orchids, the stands of white ginger, and the tall incense-smelling grasses, into the sheltering forest.

Returning to Los Angeles from our Thai/Hawaii trip, we found our landlord raising rents to "market rate" in the rather run-down so-called art colony where we'd moved to avoid the escalating greed at our old building.

Sitting next to a mountainous slag-heap of recycled concrete, this place was a nightmare of windblown dust which blanketed our cars and clogged our computers, with the added detraction of the piercing "Deet deet deet" of back-up beepers on backhoes which worked the mountain from dawn until late in the day.

In the long heat of summer, "Pork night" turned into "Pork weeks" with the stink of meat gone bad mingled with odors of rotting vegetables, when sausage makers and tomato packers in the district neglected to empty their dumpsters.

Incredibly, there was a waiting list of would-be tenants who would move in to the art colony on a moment's notice and our landlord was now renting, as often as possible, to non-artists, people with actual jobs who'd have no trouble paying much higher rents on time.

For me, this was one more exclamation point on the sentence, "Get me outta here!" Although we had a lease, hard won, which would keep us safe from unexpected expenses, it was only good for another year. After that, who knew?

We both lived and worked at home. Not going down in flames financially depended on affordable space. Common sense said we should get out from under rent, get out of L. A. altogether, and into a place of our own, and pronto.

But it was Los Angeles sculptor Yuki Oda, who probably tipped the scales for Shingo. He'd bought a house on The Big Island and had been making trips to fix it up.

He said there were so many Japanese speakers there that Shingo wouldn't have to speak "Shinglish" at all if he didn't want to. He said that many world-class artists lived and worked there, and that Shingo would be half way between the two main markets for his work, L. A. and Japan.

He said when your art wasn't selling you could go and pick coffee or bananas for $100.00 a day.

He told us that his house in Captain Cook had appreciated by a third in the year since he'd bought it. That information was less of a selling point for Shingo, who can be somewhat blind to business, but Yuki also said he planned to move there within a couple of years.

You know how, when a young woman has her first baby, her friends start wondering whether they should start a family and often do? Or, when couples get divorced, it can start a chain reaction among their friends?

Even though Oda-san's sister had told us, "Yuki? He'll never leave L. A.," Shingo began to think of The Big Island as a place where other city boys were moving: maybe he should move there, too.

8

His tone changed from "Why I need move Hawaii?" to "Something waiting us!"

And was it ever . . .

"Shingo! Shingo! I saw pigs!!!"

2

PARADISE FOUND
And It Was Green

Before we could search for and find our new home, we had to search our souls. It wasn't just a question of moving from a concrete setting to a leafy one. We had to ask ourselves whether we wanted to, whether we could, live in an unknown environment, two thousand miles of ocean away from every familiar thing, knowing very few human beings.

We were used to constant company, friends like family, dinner for twelve, with people who could understand, or pretend to understand, what Shingo was saying in his adopted language.

Many of our Downtown ex-pat friends spoke English as a language second to their native Korean, Spanish, Portugese, Farsi, Turkish, Vietnamese, or Japanese, and most of them spoke it effortlessly. But I made it clear that anyone who tried to fix "Shinglish," or made Shingo self-conscious about expressing himself was off my list.

Carl Sagan's son once said about his brilliantly articulate astronomer father, "His speech was um-less." And so was Shingo's. He got right to the point:

"I go to the my studio."

"I nose joint." (Translation: "My nose is out of joint. I'm upset.")

"I got stomach egg." (No translation needed.)

10

"I so veezy." (Busy.)

"I so exciting!"

Shingo's "Shinglish," like his beaming smile, had a purity and directness all its own.

What we did do was to teach him five-dollar English words. It became something of a game, to pick them out of the air and pass them along. One of my oldest friends, a writer, taught him "boisterous," "frugal," and "ambivalent." An ex-Playboy-bunny taught him "lascivious." A waiter "but I'm really an actor" in a Beverly Hills restaurant taught him "pretentious."

We began to realize that the words each person came up with closely described their own character. Thereafter, I was careful to teach him words that would make me look good – "patient," "generous," "evolved" – but he was onto me.

A word on both our minds was "green." We'd be greenhorns in Hawaii. We'd be outsiders who didn't know the territory, who didn't know which spider bite would require an amputation, which beach had an undertow that could drag you off to Fiji, which spot on which jungle road was armed and dangerous at marijuana picking time. Downtown street-smart wouldn't cut it. We'd both have to learn a new vocabulary.

It was going to be hard to leave the parties, which were a constant in Downtown. No need to go to bars or dance clubs for entertainment, there was usually a private party going on, through perhaps "private" doesn't exactly describe their style.

Architect Behn Samareh had to limit the guest list for his annual Downtown Hallowe'en bash to 500. The one time he didn't, it grew to 1,200 party-goers and nearly got him evicted. A sought-after invitation had people working for weeks on clever costumes, though the best I ever saw was probably made in ten minutes:

With clingwrap, a girl attached two poke-me lights, those round lamps which go on at a touch, to her teeshirt, as breasts. For her boyfriend she created a matching codpiece. Everyone wanted to "turn them on," at the risk of loud accusations of sexual harassment.

11

Our own eight-foot-tall, Buddhist inspired, hungry-ghost puppet costumes, which we operated from an inside frame, were a hit, too. With their giant heads, skinny necks, straggly hair and floppy arms, they towered over everyone, wildly gyrating on the dance floor, though, I must say, we could hardly see out of them, and nobody knew who was in there, and they were too hot.

We were going to miss the weekend camp-outs in Joshua Tree desert; the art gallery openings all over L. A.; the summer nights at California Plaza with performances and music from Brazil, or China, Guatemala, the Middle East, you name it; the casual get-togethers at Youn Woo Chaa's loft, where the table overflowed with spicy Korean food, and singers sang their newest songs, DJ's played their latest compilations, young architects, photographers, students of dance or theater showed their work to us, their most appreciative audience, and you could bring your mother.

As an only child, in Toronto, Canada, I learned early how to entertain myself, but Shingo grew up in a family of seven, in an apartment above his father's restaurant in the city of Nagaoka in northern Japan, with relatives and customers and staff coming and going day and night, and neighbors living so close by that you knew what quite a few of them looked like in their underwear. He's used to the sounds of voices and laughter and music and needs a daily dose.

Would we be lonely and lost in Hawaii? Would we be retiring from life? Shingo's answer was to start rocking in his chair like an old man on a porch. Sometimes he'd drool a little, too, for my additional amusement.

But it was my long-time dream to move to Hawaii, not his.

I'd been wishful-thinking it since the days when, as a show-runner in Hollywood, I'd spent idyllic vacations at a beach on Kauai. But the wish didn't mesh with reality: the film studios in Los Angeles where I worked weren't going to move with me.

Later, as mentioned, I tried but failed to make the move to an island, if the fun and stimulation of living in The Artists' District of Downtown L. A. can be described as failure.

12

Now was the time to go for it. But was it fair of me to push my wish on the city boy?

If he hated island life, what then? If, in the absence of distractions, he hated me, what then? Without asking directly, I wanted to know, "Do you love me enough?"

Shingo loves to say, "I love you." It's so American. In Japan, it's seldom said, especially not in public.

When we first got together, he'd go to the homes of Japanese friends, phone me, and end the call with "I love you," mostly, I'll bet, to watch the wives blush and turn away. One woman, he told me, was so embarrassed she covered her ears.

But as we made our decision to move, I had more to go on than just words. We'd lived together, and travelled together, twenty-four hours a day, seven days a week, for fifteen years, with only occasional weeks apart and only a few "I'm going to kill you!" moments.

One obvious reason for our peaceful co-existence is that we don't speak enough of each other's language. His "Shinglish" and my lack of Japanese make it difficult to fight. If one of us starts sputtering, by the time the other even begins to understand the problem, it's "Aw, forget it!" Well . . . most of the time.

Another reason is our shared religion of Zen Buddhism, through which we met, which tends to send us to our meditation cushions in times of stress or trouble, and which helps us to transcend everyday English as a means of communication.

"Everything changes," and "Be here now," are mutually held tenets, which can apply to a wrong turn on the freeway or the death of a dear friend. We could apply and rely on this shorthand as we leapt into the unknown.

But the super-glue that bonds us is humor: a must for me, the most important trait I'd want in a mate, though on first meeting Shingo Honda, I'd never have guessed it of him. Nor, as I soon learned, did he suspect it of me.

The first time we saw each other I thought, correctly, that he was a priest, this tall, skinny, straight-backed, bald-shaved guy with the shining pate and a smile to match, wearing the neat pale-blue Zen work clothes known as samu-e, who came to The Zen Center Of Los Angeles, where I was taking a sabbatical to write and study.

He thought I was almost a nun, certainly a very serious woman of Zen, since I was dressed in formal black clothing, ritually lighting incense, and preparing the zendo for meditation.

Months later, I visited his Downtown loft and discovered he was a contemporary artist, whose work had been shown at the Guggenheim Museum in New York, among many other museums, and that his Zen priesthood, though sincere, was an avocation, which he intended always to be part time, unpaid, and voluntary, not a "job."

Then he came to my second floor apartment at Zen Center. We were standing in the living room, very aware of our mutual attraction, discussing our Zen training, when I told him I had no plans to be a nun, or to write about Zen, that I was a comedy writer.

"Comedy writer? No nun? I make it terrible mistake," he said, heading for an open window, pretending to climb out of it and flee. With one leg dangling two stories above the street, he turned back to me and shrugged.

"Oh, well. Shikatanai," he said, "cannot be helped."

As I fell around laughing, he disentangled himself from the window, came back into the room and gave me a hug which still hasn't worn off.

Green: the color of money. The biggest question, as we made our decision to leave L. A., was whether we could afford to buy a house, move, and sustain ourselves on an island until we started earning income there.

Despite his friend Yuki's idea, I couldn't picture Shingo picking coffee or bananas to make money - the folks who do it are experts. And an enthusiastic audience for his new paintings would logically take time.

His last Los Angeles series of works was spare and urban in feeling, depicting people he saw on the street. He didn't know them and they didn't know each other, nor did they know they were about to interact

14

in a space of his creation, and take a trip to Japan to appear in a one-man show at the Niigata Citizen's Museum.

These painting were not instantly accepted in the city they portrayed. Curators and dealers in Los Angeles told him "People don't want to see people on their walls."

People who are supposed to know about art say some strange things about art. Haven't artists been painting people since cave-man days? Should they stop now?

Shingo knew that his work would change as his surroundings changed. In fact, his theme IS change and he didn't want to feel rushed about how he'd express it.

As for me, I'd been writing and taking photographs for a book about off-beat Downtown street gardens. More than one publisher, though interested, had said that, for retail-price reasons, they wouldn't be able to print photos of the gardens in color, only black and white. I thought a gardening book in black and white would be less than inspirational. I wanted to let the project slide until I could find a better way to bring it to life.

Here in Hawaii, there's no such thing as black and white. There's green.

From my window, I see bright green, dark green, slate green, lime green, brownish green, bluish green, shiny green, dull green: everywhere you look it's over-the-top green.

Oh, Hawaii makes a valiant try for a black and white, art film look when dark clouds pass over the sun, muting the green, graying it down. But then, as is happening right this minute, the sun comes out and the movie is once again brought to you in glorious GREEN.

Running the numbers, we believed that a move to Hawaii would give us both financial and artistic freedom, provided we made a budget and established spending priorities.

Each of us could expect some income from previous work: mine from television and music residuals, a monthly annuity, and investments in the stock market; Shingo's from the ongoing sale and rental of paintings at galleries and dealerships in Japan, New York, Los Angeles, and San Francisco.

Selling our cars, selling as much art as possible, and yard-saleing non-keepers before we left the city, together with a rent deposit rebate and loft improvements sold to our landlord, would cushion our move.

With the money from the sale of my old Kauai house, we could buy a place at a lower price and keep something in the bank. We would buy only one vehicle, a truck, until we knew what it would cost us to live.

So what did we want, individually and together, in the building and land which would be the first home we've ever lived in that we could call our own?

We agreed that access to the internet was a must for both of us, and the list went on from there:

Me – washer-dryer.

Shingo - space to make and show art.

Me - a great garden but not too much maintenance.

Shingo – near other artists.

Me – enough storage space.

Shingo – art supplies available.

Me – a pond or water feature.

Shingo – easy shipping of art.

That man! At least you know where he's coming from.

All this thinking and planning and list-making was still somewhat unreal. I can't exactly identify a moment when we said to each other, "Let's go!"

It was more an evolution as we, again, saw accomplished artist neighbors moving out of our used-to-be art colony, their lives and work disrupted, as they were priced out by higher rents, and saw and heard the new neighbors moving in, trash-talking on their cellphones in the courtyard, bragging about their plans to sell knock-off watches on the internet, putting on pay-at-the-door, pay-at-the-bar parties featuring strippers, which ended in loud drunken arguments. Though it was hard to admit it, dear old Downtown was over for us.

We went to the internet to discover what was for sale on the Hilo side of Hawaii. Searching by price, then seeing photographs, we found that the Puna District, out in the country, offered the best opportunities.

I bought a Big Island phone book and made cold calls to people in Puna to ask what they liked about living there and what they hated. It sounded as though there wasn't much to dislike except that it sometimes rained a lot.

It was cooler in parts of Puna, they said, if you lived in the mountains. "Cool," that appealed to us, since the heat of an L. A. summer was often debilitating, too hot to get anything done.

From a pie-in-the-sky list of properties which we thought we could afford, we narrowed to ten, like two lawyers choosing a jury, with each of us having a veto against qualities or characteristics which didn't suit our cause, then numbered them in order of preference, from first choice on down.

I put together a checklist of questions to ask the sellers about noise; climate; vog from the volcano; road conditions; danger from lava, landslides, earthquakes, floods, animals or humans; questions about building and garden maintenance, and where to buy groceries and other - don't forget art - supplies. We'd be able to methodically compare their answers before making any decision.

Then to the shopping trip itself: booking flights, reserving a car, buying a map-book of East Hawaii, buying a cellphone, and reserving a room at a B & B recommended by a friend, which we later referred to as "The B": it had a bed but no breakfast.

We came to The Big Island as fully prepared as any two house-hunters I've ever known, only to find, on our first full day on the island, that every single property on our list had been sold.

But by then, with the luck of the innocent, (or the ignorant), we'd already found our new home.

Shingo just called me outdoors to see an outrageous green thing. He held out a slender length of twig with a foot-long animal on it: a reptile in paddy green.

It had three horns sticking out of its chunky face, heavy lidded eyes, a low-slung body with legs that moved in deliberate slow motion, and a curly tail, wrapped around the twig for balance. It looked like a miniature brontosaurus, chopped and channeled, upholstered in embossed green vinyl, walking a tightrope.

A Jackson's chameleon? We've heard they live here. Though people keep them as pets, we returned it to the place in the bush where Shingo found it, and gently put it back where it could pretend to be a fern.

We had counted on Hawaii real estate websites to give us information, based on which we were planning to spend a lot of money. It wasn't in our plans to make several trips to The Big Island, buy several sets of tickets, rent several cars, stay in several sets of lodgings, while house-hunting. We were going to go there once, armed with all the details. We'd stay ten days, longer only if necessary. A process of elimination would reveal the best of the best. We'd make a deal and never look back, and only return to L. A. to pack.

We had no idea that houses which were on the internet for sixty or ninety days might be long gone, that it can take three months for people to do inspections and set up mortgages and that real estate is technically "available" until all the money changes hands.

And so we set out from "The B," on the first day after we arrived, list and map book in hand, to go looking, without a local realtor in tow, assuming we were in a buyers' market. Our idea was to see what we liked, then bring my friend Suzi Gillette, an island-wise real estate broker, over from Kauai to represent us and help us haggle.

On a sunny morning in March, 2005, with fluffy clouds massing in a blazing blue sky and African tulip trees blooming high and orange along the highway, we headed for Volcano Village, site of Pick Number One.

The moment we saw the town, which looked like a summer colony or a suburb, with homes built close together, our attention waned. Finding the house we'd liked in theory didn't excite us either. But parking and looking invited the interest of a neighbor, who told us she thought the house had been sold.

That was fine with us. Driving away, we agreed we didn't want to live in a village, much less one with "interested" neighbors. Hawaii, to us, was about wide-open spaces.

Our Number Two Choice was in a rural subdivision in an area called "Glenwood," which wasn't too far away. We went there next.

A newly paved thoroughfare led us off the highway to a series of sidestreets, shown in our map book as Road One, Two, Three, and so on, but we were confused – there were no street-signs.

We had to go back, start over, and count them off, until we came to Road Nine, where the house ought to be.

Though you couldn't really call it a road. It was a narrow lane, just a pair of potholed tire tracks with a strip of tallish grass down the middle. We wondered if we were in the right place, since we saw no houses at all after two quite close to corner.

We were bumping along through wilderness, forested with moss-covered ohia and primitive hapu'u fern trees, with sudden meadows of sweet-smelling grasses, spiky stands of white and purple bamboo orchids, and masses of shoulder-high ginger. Even if we were in the wrong place there was nowhere to turn around, no driveway or clearing obstructed the exuberance of nature. So we continued on.

Soon we could see the end of the road, or, at least, a place where the bush had closed over it, but still with no house in sight.

Then, surprisingly, there was a space in the overgrowth and a broad green lawn came into view. The carpet of grass rolled up to a knoll which made a stage for lacy fern trees and heart-shaped anthurium flowers, an elegant screen for the house behind it. A black lava rock driveway led to the house, which was even more appealing than it had looked on the internet.

Long and made of natural wood, it had a Japanese Zen temple feeling about it, though its metal roof and sliding glass doors used as windows were modern.

We were hesitant about driving up to the house with no appointment, but as we sat and stared from the road, the owner came out and hailed us.

"Are you house-hunting? Would you like to see the house?"

Green: the label of non-profit organizations and producers of eco-friendly products who encourage you to feel good about yourself while saving the planet, touting sustainable styles of living which reduce your yeti-size footprint on land, sea, and air. No matter where you live these days, you can't escape the message that it's better for you and everyone else if you start thinking "green."

But as we walked up to the house, I was thinking less about concept and more about color - the six green bird bums I saw sticking out of a feeder on a tree, wearing feathers of irridescent olive with undertones of black, like an Asian businessman's shot-silk suit.

"Mejiro!" Shingo recognized them immediately as birds he knew in Japan.

Can I call it love at first sight? We'd had photographs of this house, which we'd downloaded off the internet, on file for almost four months.

We'd seen pictures of it inside and out. We knew its square footage; how much the taxes were; that it had two bedrooms, a modern kitchen with as-new appliances, and one and three quarters baths; that it had two wood burning stoves, laminated wood flooring, Berber carpet, and a mother-in-law suite, which, in Hawaii, can be euphemism for "rooms to rent out."

We knew that it was "off the grid," one reason why its asking price was cheaper than if it had all the utilities, though, admittedly, we were naive about what that meant.

If not in love, we were certainly in like. Our faces showed it, but as potential buyers, we tried to conceal our enthusiasm.

Unlike most developers, the owner-builder hadn't bulldozed the land and flattened every growing thing. He'd cleared by hand just enough space to make his home, then worked with the native fern trees and tall ohias and mysterious mosses, to create a series of beauty spots which he manicured, adding other exotic plants. These garden islands were surrounded by lawns, but one sixth of his half-acre was still jungle-wild and untouched.

The house was built to take advantage of the views, with sliding glass doors on both sides of each of the main rooms, bringing outdoors in. A screened lanai, and a little pond with darting goldfish (a water feature!) added charm. A huge covered woodpile with perfectly cut, sorted, and stacked logs at the back of the property promised cozy warmth on cool nights.

We couldn't help congratulating the man on his building and landscaping and wood-chopping skills. The more we saw, the more impossible it was to be poker-faced. We understood his pride in the place and why "he ambivalent," to quote Shingo, about moving to Florida.

He told us the property had actually been sold several months ago. He'd already moved his furniture to Sarasota when the deal fell apart over financing. In the meantime, he'd bought a house there and now couldn't follow through. We realized we were his ideal buyers because we intended to pay cash and could close escrow in thirty days.

Green: the skin-tone of seven frogs who live in our water-feature. In the daytime, they sit for hours on the lava rocks surrounding the pond, fully aware, not sleeping, not blinking, not moving a muscle. We call them "Sensei" – teacher - for their high-level instruction in meditation technique.

The biggest, greenest frog we call "Roshi" - Zen master. But when he flops into the pond, as he just did, and lies there, legs splayed, uttering croaks of desire to a purple water lily, it kind of ruins his image. Shingo has renamed him, "Lascivious Roshi."

The owner of the house went on to tell us about living off the grid. He'd installed only two solar panels, which ran the pump for the water system and the lighting in the house. There was a back-up generator that he used for his power tools. He said he went to bed when the sun went down so he didn't need much electricity. If we bought the house, he thought we'd need at least two more solar panels and four more batteries to be able to run additional lights and whatever else we needed.

He showed us the propane tanks that powered the kitchen range, refrigerator, and water heater, and told us that filling them just meant a quick trip to a local gas station.

He said he'd had a washer and dryer that he shipped to Florida. If we wanted to install laundry equipment, we'd need to use the generator.

"I used to just put it on, start the washer, go do my grocery shopping, and when I came back the laundry was done," he said.

He showed us the plentiful water supply in its "catchment tank," an above-ground swimming pool with a tent-like top, which caught and stored rainwater from gutters around the roof.

A solar-powered water pump, a pressure tank, two simple filters, and the propane-fired on-demand water heater delivered hot and cold water to the house. We'd have to buy drinking water unless we installed special filters to make the water potable, but drinking water was cheap and easy to find.

He showed Shingo under the house so he could see the quality of construction and the wiring layout. He showed us the cesspool and the plumbing for it.

We went through our list of buyer's questions and were satisfied with his answers.

We'd have peace and quiet since nobody else lived on the street except for one nice lady at the corner and some renters in the second house we'd seen. There were neighbors on other sideroads, but we'd never notice, since his property was deeply buffered by woods.

There was no danger from flooding because the land sloped away from the house which was built on piers. There was no danger of forest fires because the climate was too wet. Because of its mountain elevation, no lava could flow to the house from the active volcano, Kilauea, to the south - lava can't flow uphill. As for vog, the smelly sulphuric gas that often escaped from the volcano, he said the house was in a spot with the right prevailing winds so that vog rarely if ever penetrated.

Animals? There were songbirds, doves, native pheasants, and owls, in the area. And there were wild pigs, but they weren't likely to come around the house with people living there. There were no coqui frogs, a noisy local nuisance.

There could be no television without a dish. Because there was no phone line there could be no cable TV, and the internet was only available by wireless which he didn't know anything about. He used a cellphone and had no trouble with reception.

There was no postal delivery but the post office was only a few miles away and UPS and Fedex would deliver to the door.

There was no garbage pick-up, you had to go to the dump, but the dump was on the way to the post office.

You had to do your own road maintenance, bringing crushed rock up by truck and filling potholes but you might only need to do it every year or two - our hosts at "The B" had told us they had to do the same. He used a gardener to cut the grass and had him weed-whack out on the road as well.

As to weather in a tropical rainforest, we could count on some rain most days, which meant we'd rarely have to water the garden, though there was usually a dry spell twice a year. Often it rained at night and the days were sunny, much like the March weather we'd been having since we arrived. Because it was cooler in the mountains, there were fewer bugs.

For supplies he went to Hilo, where everything he needed was available. Art supplies? He didn't know, but probably.

By this time our heads were spinning with too much information. We thanked him for the tour, told him we were interested, but that this was the first house we'd seen. We took his phone number. We'd look at other houses and then be in touch.

As we walked out into the driveway, a showy planting of lipstick red anthuriums caught my eye, and one mauve orchid growing out of a hapu'u fern tree. I pictured the orange and pink tropicals I'd add to the mix, the bananas and pineapples I'd plant in the front yard. I didn't dare look at Shingo until we were in the car and on our way. Could he see himself living there as I was already doing?

"That us's house," he said before we were even out of the driveway.

"Could be," I said, trying to keep calm.

But the message of "the greens" had definitely found its mark. Maybe I'd read one too many "green" books, catalogues, and magazines, which I used to pore over, even living in our gritty Downtown lofts. Notions of moving off the grid had been percolating under my L. A. surface, like the Hawaiian Goddess Pele's hot volcanic magma.

Free electricity from the sun. Free water from the sky. Heat from your own woods. Grow what you eat. Preserve what you don't. Raise a few chickens, but just for the eggs. Compost the kitchen scraps. Reduce, recycle, re-use. Self-sufficiency. Sustainability. Living off the land. In a RAINFOREST (buzzword, buzzword). I may have enthused about such things as we drove away.

Of course, we agreed, you can't buy the first house you see. You have to, you must, you'd be foolish not to do comparison shopping. You might find something you liked even better. We hurried back to "The B" and called a local realtor to make appointments for the next day. That's when we got the news that every other place on our list was gone.

"Everything changes," I reminded myself as I asked for a new list in our price range in Puna, telling the agent we'd drive by anything available starting in the morning, then called our broker-friend Suzi Gillette on Kauai asking her to come to The Big Island as soon as possible.

"Be here now," no need to say it, just do it: we re-organized on the spot, looking up new addresses in our map book, planning our route.

By late the following morning we were on the road. By early evening we were back at "The B." We'd seen nine properties and been completely under-whelmed. There wasn't one house we wanted to see more of, not one that called to us or seemed to have possibilities. "Us's house" put them all in the shade.

That night, another couple at "The B" related their house-hunting horrors. They said the housing market on Hawaii was so hot that people were overbidding asking prices. They'd lost two potential homes to higher bidders before having an offer accepted. Even so, they were nervous because there were backup offers waiting: any slip in their obligations could sink their deal. We realized we needed expert help immediately, called Suzi, and asked her to, "Get here now."

Things moved quickly after that.

Suzi and her husband Richard, a builder, came, saw, and approved of the house. They asked the seller and his realtor questions we didn't know enough to ask, and saw us though the innumerable details of decision-making. Well within our ten-day timetable, after offers and counter-offers, we bought our home, paying slightly more than we'd expected. Then it was back to Los Angeles to endure the escrow period, wind up our affairs, pack, and move.

Did we buy the place in too big a rush? Probably.

Were we under too much pressure? Perhaps.

But love is love. You have to live it or you might be missing something, right?

Which is why we were soon to find ourselves up the creek, er, off the grid without a paddle.

There's a green here in Hawaii that I haven't described. It's a very muddy green that happens when pigs come to dine in your garden, leaving sideways pineapple plants, upside down bananas, chomped-on flowers, and great, deep, swaths carved out of the lawn.

We discovered, a moment ago, that pigs came to a five-course dinner of yummy worms and delectable roots last night, leaving their earthy stamp on the verdant green.

Again!

3

AUGUST IN PARADISE
Trust

You need trust to make a long distance move, especially when you're moving off the grid: trust in people and the information they give you. Your lifestyle, and even your life, depends on it. How soon you learn, sometimes at great expense, that most of the information you get will be wrong.

As in:

"Your move will cost about eight thousand dollars."

"Your belongings will arrive in three weeks."

"Your Puna neighborhood is cool."

"It mostly rains at night and the days are sunny."

"Verizon serves your neighborhood."

"You can get wireless internet."

"You can install a washer and dryer and run them off the generator."

"You've got a great little generator, there."

"You'll probably need two more solar panels."

"You'll only need to fix the road every couple of years."

"Pigs aren't likely to come around with people living in the house."

"There are no noisy coqui frogs."

But I'm getting ahead of my story . . .

It had been three months since our house-hunting trip. Though we'd formally owned our piece of paradise since the end of April, we gave ourselves plenty of time in L. A. to sell up and pack up and go.

First we contacted Shingo's art dealers to let them know we were leaving. They could come to our studio and choose work to keep on consignment. After they'd made their selections, we held an open studio for three weeks, contacting his private collectors. It had that last chance feeling as people came in to add to their art collections.

Next "to do" was a yard sale, set up on a work-table in the courtyard outside our door. "Nothing Over $3.00," said the sign and people got good bargains: last year's sequined Halloween costumes, vintage vinyl records, ski-clothes, books, excess electronics, things we could do without or couldn't use in Hawaii. At night, I put a floodlight above the table, so art colony neighbors could shop until midnight, sliding their dollar bills under our door if it was closed or stopping in to chat if it wasn't. We pretty much sold out, though I did spot Shingo slipping quite a few things off the table, sneaking them back into the studio, and packing them.

It would be an anticlimax to leave L. A. without giving a party to say so-long and thanks for all the good times. Ours was staged early, with an eye to the exhaustion factor, three weeks before we exited, in our own and a neighbor's lofts, with performances and DJs alternating in both. Talented friends, and total strangers performed and made music for dancing. Though many of our oldest chums had left the city, around 150 people came. That's Downtown.

But then there were the "Oh my God, you're going so far away" dinners, the "Have a great life!" visits, and the last-night-in-L. A. get-together at Youn Woo Chaa's with our nearest and dearest, once all our things were taken away by the movers.

We dragged ourselves to it, to find that Cita, singer/songwriter without peer - on her website a Mexican poet exclaims, "After I heard Cita, I never slept again"; her "boyfriend-for-life" Ricardo Ochoa, guitarist from heaven; Carmen Zella, grant-winning video artist and sometime clarinet player; Mark Scully, all-star human and mostdanceable DJ; and Youn Woo Chaa, that wild Korean who went to the Amazon to discover himself and came back to create art that is making him famous, including a portrait of Shingo Honda woven in cane, collected by the Korean National Contemporary Museum, had written and recorded a song for us:

"Shingo and Lynne are going to a beautiful island across the sea," they sang, "across the sea, across the sea . . . across the street!"

None of us said goodbye. That would be silly.

Finally, on the first of August, we were here, "across the street," on The Big Island, ready to start The Big Adventure.

I'd booked two nights for us at a hotel in Hilo so we'd have time to learn how to run the new house, with its unfamiliar solar panels, generator, and propane appliances, before actually moving in. Arriving in balmy Hilo at night, we checked in to the hotel, and barely managed to unpack our toothbrushes before we were sound asleep.

Sunrise greeted us in the morning with pink and golden skies over azure Hilo Bay, but we didn't hurry out of bed, letting ourselves relax and unwind after the stress and tight schedule of leaving Downtown and the logyness of jet lag. We dawdled over breakfast in the open-air hotel dining room to the sound of the ocean lapping the shore, feeling the warmth of the day, liking our state of limbo, not quite ready to take on responsibility.

We had to remind ourselves that we weren't tourists, not just visitors to Hawaii, though in some sense we all are.

We were land-owners now – but no, that didn't work either: no one can really own the land, it doesn't belong to us, as Madame Pele has pointed out to people over and over by covering what they thought they owned with lava.

Driving to our new home, we decided to think of ourselves in the Hawaiian way, as "people who belong to the land."

We rode up Highway 11 with the windows of our rental-car rolled down, seeing again the lush forests, the miles of flowers, the open fields surrounding cute communities, remarking over the lack of traffic, the clean smell of the air, and the sudden drop in temperature.

At 2,000 feet above sea level, near the village of Mountain View, the air suddenly cooled, as though we'd stepped from a hot city street into an air-conditioned store.

Our neck-of-the-woods, further up the highway, was even cooler. Not cold, we assured each other, just a little nippy, roll-up-the-windows nippy, perhaps because it had been raining. Judging from deep pools of water in the low spots on the access road, it must have been raining hard.

Once again we turned onto Road Nine, with its meadows and trees and orchids and ginger, freshly washed and glistening from the rain. Its potholes, filled with puddles, were of unknown depth, but we made it through them, splashing along to nowhere.

"Us's house," though we knew it was there, seemed so far away. We each felt a twinge of the doubt and desolation you get in lonely places but smiled our way out of it.

Our first sight of the house was a thrill. At the same time we were anxious. We'd naturally worried about break-ins or vandalism with the place being empty for so long, but the former owner had installed a well-tried local security system, a chain across the road which prevented a view of the house with a sign on it saying, "Beware Of The Dog."

Dogs on the Island of Hawaii are usually not toy poodles They're beasts of the rottwieler, pit bull, tear a hunk out of a pig, tear a hunk out of you if you get in my way, type. So a sign to "Beware" is taken seriously.

We'd been told, by Suzi Gillette, our real estate angel, that there'd been pig damage to the lawns during the summer, but, having hired Twin Brothers' First Rate Yard Care long-distance out of the Hawaii Yellow Pages, we found everything picture perfect – lawns neatly trimmed, trees looking ferny, and flowers greeting us with friendly faces.

After fumbling with the new set of keys to the front door, we danced through the empty rooms, then wandered to the back garden. Even the goldfish in the little pond were alive and well and frisky.

29

An inflatable bed and bedclothes, a sleeping bag, some pots, pans, cutlery, and cleaning supplies had been left in the house for us. By adding things we'd brought in our luggage, and doing some minimal shopping, we could camp there in relative comfort until the moving van arrived.

Our assignment, that first day, was to find out how to turn on the propane refrigerator, and the on-demand propane hot-water heater; how to use the inverter for the electrical system; and how to know at what point we should use the generator.

The kitchen range ran on propane but used electricity to fire the burners and the oven. We noticed that the plug had been left out of its outlet and wondered whether or not to plug it in.

A voluminous packet of information, neatly filed according to subject, had also been left for us. I searched through pertinent files - Shingo doesn't read much English - labeled "Refrigerator," "Water Heater," "Inverter," "Generator," and "Range," but couldn't zero in on specifics. It was like getting five new computers at once and trying to make sense of the owner's manuals.

After a few failed tries at starting the fridge, I called the seller's real estate agent and asked him to come and help us, never thinking he'd come right away. But he did.

To make the call I'd had to walk out into the road. I couldn't seem to get a cellphone connection from anywhere inside the house. Odd, because I'd had no trouble reaching the seller when I called, while house-hunting, from "The B." This was something to be concerned about, but not now. There were too many other things to think about.

Within an hour the agent had arrived and shown us how to start the propane appliances – not hard to do, just new to us.

He then took us outside and demonstrated how to tell how much propane was in the tanks, one for the kitchen appliances and one for the water heater. You could lift them up and shake them a little to hear how much liquid you had left. This sounded fine to Shingo but I couldn't lift the big one. I put "tank" on my mental look-into-it list, right next to "What's with the cellphone?"

30

While we were out at the side of the house, he showed us the volt-meter for the solar panels and how to understand it.

A needle pointed to a color, either yellow, green, or red. If the needle slipped into the yellow zone we needed to charge the batteries.

To do this we were supposed to connect a portable battery charger to the generator and hook it up to the battery bank, just as you'd do if you were trying to jump-start a car.

The battery charger and the generator itself had been left inside the house to guard against theft. We decided that tomorrow would be soon enough to take them out and try them.

For the inverter, which turned solar energy into usable power, the agent said it was a good idea to reach under the kitchen sink and turn it off when we retired at night so that energy didn't "leak." Not realizing that meant we'd have to use a flashlight to find our way to bed, I said, "Okay."

As he left, our gentle and gentlemanly instructor, it started to rain. I offered to see him to his car with my big umbrella, but he almost scoffed at the idea.

"It's always raining here," he said. "We call it liquid sunshine. Nobody bothers with an umbrella." And out he went, without hurrying, though it began to pour.

We decided to leave too, after making a list of food and necessities we'd need to buy before spending our first night at the house.

We'd go back to the hotel, have an excellent dinner in their dining room, and enjoy the ocean until bedtime. We'd call from the beach to our friends "across the street" to let them know how well things were going. Tomorrow, we'd be moving in!

"Coqui! Coqui!" We didn't hear the coqui frog that first afternoon as we walked to the car, but I can hear him now.

He's a tiny tree frog, the scourge of The Big Island.

He has a piercing two-tone whistle which sounds like his name: "Coqui! Coqui!" But loud. If there's one around you know it. If there are hundreds, you'd better buy a ticket to somewhere else, or consider suicide: you won't be able to hold a quiet conversation, listen to your favorite music, hear the dialogue in a movie, or get any sleep, since the coqui starts to belt it out in the early evening and doesn't quit 'til dawn.

But, in that first gathering dusk, either he didn't sing or we didn't hear him as we set off to be pampered for one last night in Hilo.

The next day was a busy one, no lollygagging.

After breakfast, we checked out of the hotel, and found our way around Hilo for shopping errands. We didn't make it back to the house until after lunch.

It was a warm blue-sky day and we didn't think to bring logs in for the woodstoves right away. Groceries were unpacked and stored, and decisions made about where to eat and sleep.

We'd bought two cheap lounge chairs which Shingo flattened into a low table base in the otherwise empty living room, using found left-over wood to create a temporary table top. We'd have to dine sitting on the floor as some people still do in Japan, but it would be comfortable, the floor was carpeted.

We made up the inflatable bed, left behind for us, in the "mother-in-law" space, which had sliding glass doors on both sides and its own small wood-burning stove. From our bed we could gaze at a crackling fire or look out at the trees and the stars.

We decided which closets to use for our clothes, who got which drawers in the bathroom, and did some unpacking of luggage.

By then it was getting dark. We switched on a few lights in the house and went outside to the solar meter.

Whoa! With just the kitchen and bathroom lights on we were using up all our electricity.

We had to be sure we had enough for the water pump, which, we quickly discovered, went on with a noisy "Brrrrrrrrrrr" every time we used the toilet, and again when we washed our hands, and again when we ran water in the kitchen: an annoying sound, grounds for another mental note.

It was also getting chilly. And it had started to rain.

Wood! We needed wood to be warm. The wood was in the wood-pile down at the back of the property. We had only one umbrella and no carry-sling for the logs. Shingo was elected to make trips back and forth to bring enough wood for the night. I'd receive it at the door and stack it by the fireplaces. Each of us would then start a fire in one of the stoves.

Burning wood from the land we belonged to: how self-sufficient can you be? Ohia and guava hardwood had been cut to perfect size and well seasoned in the woodpile, but it wasn't exactly dry. A rainforest, we were learning, is a world of pervading damp.

Starting the fires became a competition. Each of us used our favorite camping techniques to get a fire going. I preferred the square stacking of kindling and logs, while Shingo liked a teepee look. But the moment one of us gloated about our ability, intending to show the other a roaring fire, we'd glance back to find it had gone out. Much trading of know-how went on, extra kindling was hunted down, and every available scrap of paper and wooden match was readied for use. Result: two beautiful fires. And two ravenously hungry fire builders.

Okay. Dinner. The kitchen range needed electricity to fire the oven, but the burners would light just as well with a lighter. We decided we shouldn't use more electricity than absolutely necessary because the generator and battery charger were still sitting inside the house. Though the charger was on wheels, the generator wasn't and it weighed a ton. We'd have to deal with it next day, hopefully in the sun. Until tomorrow, we'd leave the plug for the stove out of its receptacle, use a lighter to fire the burners, and turn off the kitchen lights as soon as possible.

Candles, newly purchased, on the "table," and a flashlight aimed at the ceiling, gave us romantic light for dinner. A portable radio, left for us by the thoughtful former owner, we tuned to Hawaiian music.

Seared mahi mahi with a salad of sliced avocado, onion, and tomatoes, tasted fine and looked colorful served on bright yellow plastic plates. Shingo, who can't live without rice, had brought campers' boil-in-the-bag, which we prepared in a pot on the stove in the absence of a rice- cooker.

After dinner it was hula time. We definitely needed lessons. And we needed more wood and kindling. Both fires were out again.

High on the newness, we went back into the fray, adding wood, standing watch, fussing and poking at every ember. Our first lesson in interdependence: we needed a fire and a fire needed a friend.

By 10:00 PM we were wiped out and ready for bed, when I remembered I'd better turn off the inverter under the kitchen sink, forgot that it turned off all the electricity in the house, didn't take a flashlight, and got stranded, trying to feel my way out of the pitch-dark kitchen, until Shingo came, flashlight in hand, to lead me through the darkened house, past low-flickering fires, into the mother-in-law suite, our spacious new bedroom.

We'd been adding layers of clothing throughout the evening, having not yet adjusted to Hawaii's mountain night-time temperature. Wearing sweatpants and sweatshirts, we were reluctant to take them off and got into bed fully clothed. Using the sleeping bag we'd found as a blanket, we snuggled in but couldn't sleep.

Beyond the windows the sky was black, that black black you never see in the city. A blaze of stars came out of hiding as clouds blew by. Mars, the Red Planet, was really red, flashing coded messages to the universe. And the rising moon backlit drops of rain in the trees, turning the scene outside our windows into a sparkling fairyland.

We had to jump up, grab flashlights, and go outside, sitting on the back steps to take it all in.

As though some unseen hand had strung tiny Christmas lights in every tree, as if the world convention of fireflies had decided to meet in our backyard, the forest twinkled and glowed. Each frond of each hapu'u fern tree wore a diamond necklace; each leaf of ohia displayed a pearl.

We clung to each other, shivering with awe, then just plain shivering, acknowledging that it really was quite cool at night. Not cold. It wasn't cold. After all, this was August and this was the tropics. It couldn't be cold, could it?

Shingo, whose normal body temperature is lower than mine, is often shivering when I'm not. But whether it was or wasn't cold, I noticed he put on yet another layer of clothing after we came indoors, and bounced around in our inherited air-bed adjusting his wads of insulation before lapsing into dreams.

"Coqui!" The coqui frog is an unintended import from the Caribbean to Hawaii where it has no natural enemies and feels free to breed like a rabbit on Viagra.

Puerto Ricans adore the little tree frog, which is about the size of your thumbnail, but Hawaiians hate and revile it: it's taking over their island.

Suzi Gillette had suggested in March that we go to the house at night to hear whether we had coquis. "Due diligence" it's called in the real estate business. But on our house-hunting trip we'd decided to spend our last day at the beach, and frankly, couldn't be bothered. Leaving in the morning, what could we do about it anyway? We were happy to take the seller's word that there were none in the area.

"Coqui! Coqui!" But there is one now. He lives in a fern tree bordering our front lawn. Was he here last spring when we bought the house? We'll never know and we don't care. We like this frog. We need this frog. He's our only neighbor.

Awakening for the first time in our new home, we expected an opalescent dawn like the ones we'd enjoyed in Hilo, viewed from the third floor of our cushy hotel. But morning at our place was all about rain. Not a gentle rain which blesses the trees and flowers, but a downpour, a deluge, pelting, pounding, blowing out of a charcoal sky.

It was only 5:30 AM but we couldn't sleep because of the noise. I should say noises, all of them new to us. Water gurgled through the eavestroughs on its way to the catchment tank. Water dripped off forty-foot-tall ohia trees and splatted onto the metal roof. Water sheeted off the roof in places, making waterfalls, and bounced wherever it landed.

35

"This Hawaii?" said Shingo. "I freezing."

"Me too," I had to admit it.

"Okay," he said, "Vacation over. Go home."

We were well into a mock fight over who had to give up the relative warmth of our bed and get up and make the tea, when we noticed that it was both raining and sunny at the same time.

In our backyard, golden light from the rising sun played on silver veils of rain. Across from our front yard, above the trees, against a canvas of steel gray clouds, we could see a double rainbow forming.

Once again, we were out of bed and out the door in minutes, marvelling as the rain and sun completed their watercolor painting in the sky.

"A double rainbow. Lucky!" I exclaimed to Shingo.

"Irashai, welcome, say," he concurred, as he gave the rainbow a bow of appreciation.

But then it was back to reality as we started our off the grid day. Did we have enough electricity to run our brand new $12.00 Walmart toaster? No. We needed sun for the solar panels, but the sun had been and gone. Liquid sunshine flowed from the sky, but from it no voltage flowed.

I made grilled cheese sandwiches using the kitchen stove, and they were good, but, if it's toast you want, you want your toast.

This had to be the day to find out how to use the generator. Without it we couldn't even turn on the lights in the house: according to the voltmeter we didn't have enough power.

Out came the manual for the generator and we studied, in the semi-darkness, for a while. Shingo, the artist, is more visually oriented. He was able to understand, from drawings, how to make it go. I relate better to the written word and got other instructions: like, you have put gas in it, you have put oil in it, both of which we located, left for us under the house.

Now we had to move the heavy thing outdoors. It had to slide down the stairs from the kitchen and be hauled into the carport, passing through puddles and mud. But somehow, the muddiness helped. The generator slipped and slid into place without either of us having to call a chiropractor.

Next, we needed to understand the battery charger, which was going to carry electricity fifteen feet from the generator in the carport to the battery bank in a cupboard at the side of the house. Shingo knew how to connect it to the batteries from many years of jump-starting his old Mitsubishi van in L. A., but I was afraid he might get an electric shock since he was going to hook up in the rain.

He decided to connect the battery charger fully before starting the generator. Then it would be a simple matter of one, two, three, four.

One: turn it on. Two: engage the choke. Three: pull the starter cord. Four: push the choke lever to "run" and hear the generator kick into life. That first time, though, it was more like one, two, three, three, three, three, three, three, with so many pulls of the starter cord. This generator, like an aging chorus girl, couldn't be counted on to kick to the beat. But finally it started up, with a cloud of black exhaust and a deafening roar.

One of the main selling points of our newly purchased half-acre of utopia was the enveloping peace and quiet, now shattered by this diabolically noisy machine. Who told us it was a "great little generator"? Not! Were we going to have to hear this racket every time we wanted to eat a piece of toast or read a book?

And were we going to have to put on rubber boots and run around in the mud to hook up and start and stop the thing?

That was unthinkable. We'd surely have lots of sun. Why else would a longtime Puna resident and knowledgeable builder, Mr. Off The Grid himself, who'd lived in and so reluctantly sold us the house, have installed a solar system? We had the budget for two more solar panels and the additional storage batteries he'd recommended. The generator was for "backup." We wouldn't be needing it that much.

But until the moving van arrived we couldn't enlarge the system. To assess our needs or hire a contractor, all our electronics, small appliances, and lighting should be in place. We'd been told we'd have to count the watts and amperes and volts they used, though the very idea had eyes rolling up into heads – electrical engineers we're not, and, by the way, what's a watt?

There was no choice but to make do with the piddly two panels, the pain-in-the-butt battery charger, and the roaring generator, until our forty-foot container arrived. That's right, I said forty-foot container. Well, you can't sell EVERYTHING! Some things you might need in Hawaii.

"Coqui! Coqui!" It's sunset time. Our little neighbor just welcomed us as we came home from the beach. He sang to us last night when we walked out to see the moon. "Co-qui!" He whistles the bottom and top notes of an octave, and I whistle back, "Co-qui!"

Sometimes I try to make him sing another song, or a variation of "Coqui!" by whistling other notes in other tempos: a blues riff or a few bars of salsa. But the little guy sticks to his tune, never changing. If he did, he probably wouldn't attract a mate. That's the reason for his two-note serenade.

Our next priority was to buy a truck. We'd only booked a rental car for a week. But one day stretched into another as we set up bank accounts and grocery shopped, signed in at the post office, and discovered that the local library went way beyond books - you could use the internet for free and rent DVD's for a dollar a week; as we topped up the propane tanks, bought gas for the generator, bought drinking water, went to the laundromat to wash our clothes, and to the "transfer station" to discard our garbage, finding it to be the most beautiful dump on earth, with bamboo and wildflowers growing all around, and wild chickens clucking as you threw away your trash. We had to re-up the rental car for another week before we got our act together.

Meanwhile, there was the cellphone.

"Can you hear me now?" Nope.

Used to a land-line, I'd bought the cellphone in L. A. for our house-hunting trip with a prepaid calling card, hoping to avoid the unexpected charges friends had warned about.

The people who ran the store couldn't guarantee much about reception on The Big Island, which was just a dot on their map without a hint of detail. I crossed my fingers and bought the package. And calls from sea level on Hawaii Island worked fine. But to get or make a phonecall in the mountains we were having to walk out into the road.

Calls from the house faded or were cut off in mid-sentence, which is manageable when you're calling friends, you just call them back, but not when you're in the middle of one of those Press 1, Press 2, Press 6, already frustrating conversations with a machine – downright scary when it's a machine at your bank and you're trying to transfer funds to cover a check that's already out there against an account that's going to bounce it.

Calls from our back steps got us nowhere because there was a roof overhead. So it was out and away to the road, place the call, punch a bunch of buttons ("To transfer funds, Press 9") in the liquid sunshine, while adjusting an umbrella to improve reception.

Liquid sunshine: we had to learn to live with it. Day after day it mostly rained, though the sun, like a faithless lover, would occasionally drop by to tantalize, then go on to another tryst.

We learned not to wait around for it, and not to let the weather put a damper on our plans: to go snorkeling at the marine sanctuary in the rain, swimming in the hot pond in the rain, visit a botanical garden in the rain, see the volcano in the rain, hike up the road into the wilderness in the rain.

If it was raining, we'd go anyway, and see mercury puddles on a broad-leafed plant, feel cool needles on our faces as we floated in warm water, see new variations of the color black on wet lava, and smell the freshly-washed earthiness of the Island of Hawaii that we couldn't stop hungrily inhaling.

We went to Hilo in the rain and bought our truck, a 4X4 used Mazda with extra-cab and a campershell. If it hadn't been raining I doubt we'd have understood how useful that campershell would be: we could see that truckbeds without them were awash in water despite their drainholes. The rain helped us decide to spend a little more than

39

planned for the extra-cab feature, too. That space would be good for hauling propane tanks. They could be quickly strapped into the jump-seats with seatbelts, rather than roping them into the bed of the truck in a downpour. We'd need those two extra seats for guests, too, when they stopped by from "across the street."

Four-wheel drive was indispensable for faraway places, like the spectacular Champagne Ponds, a geothermal lagoon, where the rutted, potholed mud-on-lava access road was impassable without it. With the amount of rain we were getting, our own street, Road Nine, soon fell into that category: puddles grew into ponds as the rains washed potholes even deeper.

We began to be concerned that the moving van, which should be delivering our belongings any moment, might have trouble making it up Road Nine. A wrecked sports-pickup carelessly parked half-on, half-off, the shoulder would add to the difficulty.

So it was out in the rain with the cellphone trying to find out who owned the truck, and out in the rain with the cellphone to get a firm delivery date from our mover.

As it turned out, there was no need to worry or hurry. Our L. A. mover couldn't locate our container. It had been lost in transit.

"Coqui! Coqui!" Shingo and I have been thinking about the future and how our tree-frog neighbor fits into it.

We only have one coqui now, and it's the male who sings. The girls are apparently primping underground, waiting for the boys to call. They say one coqui girlfriend can lay thirty eggs, which all hatch with no predator to eat them, and that, before we know it, there could be a chorus of coquis, a coqui choir, a coqui National Symphony. Soon, the entire forest could be infested the way it is on other parts of the island. This one little frog, like Adam, could be the progenitor of unimaginable numbers.

As "people who belong to the land" we must be responsible stewards. We can't just hang out with this frog. We have to consider murder. But from what I've heard, coqui killing may be easier said than done.

In Volcano Village the other day I saw a gorgeous red camellia bush covered with white powder. It looked as though somebody had thrown on a five-pound sack of a lime. I'm guessing this was assault with intent to kill a coqui. Why else would anyone make such a mess of their tree?

A new friend, ceramic artist Clayton Amemiya, who has a shop in Hilo, told us he was closing early. He had to get home to cut down a tree which housed, guess what? a coqui.

At the post office, a woman told us about her brother's best-friend's wife's highly successful coqui extermination system:

Around sunset she sneaks out silently and waits at the base of a tree where a frog has been heard to sing. She's wearing one rubber glove and carrying a flashlight, which she doesn't yet turn on.

As the sun wanes, the coqui chirps, revealing his hiding place. Dark descends, and he begins to climb the tree. Patiently squatting, she waits, and waits, then pounces.

Mesmerizing the frog with her flashlight, she grabs him in her gloved hand, pulls the rubber glove inside out, and traps the frog. She then puts the gloved frog in her freezer, where he dies an Arctic death.

"All this is for one frog?" I asked the lady at the post office.

"Yeah. But she's caught three of 'em so far."

You really don't want to yell at your mover. They've got all your worldly possessions and you don't. But how can you LOSE a forty-foot container? I found it hard to keep my voice level while asking this question.

Many liquid sunshine phone calls later I learned that you lose it by sending it to Honolulu instead of Hilo, and that it then has to come by barge to its correct destination, and, of course, that takes time. How much time depends on when a barge is coming to The Big Island and whether it has room for a forty-foot container. So maybe ten days, maybe two weeks longer we'd be camping in an empty house.

"Things change." "Be here now." Again we relied on our principles, realizing how lucky we were, two immigrants to the United

States from Canada and Japan, to have an empty house, with food on a makeshift table, wood in a woodpile, and fireplaces to burn it in.

Sitting on the floor, in candlelight, over dinner, we talked about the Japanese cane workers, among other earlier immigrants, who came to Hawaii with nothing, not expecting any forty-foot container.

And their children, Japanese Americans, some of whom lost everything they'd worked for when they were rounded up and sent to internment camps after Japan dropped bombs on Pearl Harbor.

And the many internees, brave men, boys really, who volunteered to fight and die in World War II, determined to prove their loyalty to the country they were born in, for the sake of their families and future generations. We'd met some of them, in their eighties now, at the Café 100 in Hilo, which is named for the Japanese-American 100th Infantry Battalion, the most decorated unit in U.S. military history for its size and length of service. Without them, and their unimaginable sacrifices, our life on this island might not have been possible. We found ourselves with tears in our eyes, and not because our stuff was in Honolulu.

Today I read in the paper that the coqui frog has been declared "a noxious pest" by the Government of Hawaii. This means that officials bent on frogicide can go onto private land without trespassing and send coquis to kingdom come, using poison sprays or other weapons of frog destruction. Right now, however, there aren't enough of said "officials" to make much of a dent in the problem. And there isn't enough money to hire more of said "officials."

But money has been found to educate the public about the frog. I now know how to make a coqui trap.

You take a length of bamboo and drill a 1" hole toward the bottom of it, slice off the top and make a rain repellent roof out of a piece of plastic bag attached with a rubber band. The coqui male will use this refuge to mate with his lady-friend. After she lays her eggs, she goes back into the ground while he sits in the bamboo tube and guards the eggs. It's your job to check the trap every now and then to see if he's in there with his brood.

42

Now wait a minute! The coqui frog is a house-husband??? You want me to slay this feminist frog?

Mr. Off The Grid, Mr. Self-Sufficiency, who built our house, had told us that he got up at dawn and went to sleep soon after dark. And now we knew why. Because he didn't have any lights. He'd installed them in the bathrooms and kitchen, but he had to run the evil-sounding generator if he wanted them to work.

We fell into a pattern of running it at sundown, just as the coqui began to sing.

Each and every time, Shingo had to set up the battery charger between the generator and the battery bank. Almost always, he had to do it in the rain, but I never heard a swear-word out of him.

Yes, we've all taught him choice obscenities, in English, Korean, Spanish, whatever – five-dollar expletives, of course. His favorite is colorfully Korean and means "You are a rat's private parts," but you don't dare say it to anyone Korean unless you'd like a bloody nose.

If you asked him today why he was so stoic about the ridiculous electrical set-up, he'd tell you it was because he (we) didn't know it could be any different. "Shikatanai, cannot be helped," was his motto.

His uncomplaining acceptance of the daily battery charger/generator insanity gave us voltage, over and above what we needed for the water pump, to turn on lights while making dinner, with enough left over to run them again while doing the dishes, and with, maybe, some left over for reading a newspaper or magazine.

To read at night I'd push the inflatable bed up next to the mother-in-law bathroom to shed some light on the subject, but often used a flashlight if we got low on energy. After 8:00 PM it was too late to run the generator again: sound carries for miles in the countryside at night.

Flashlights and candles were an important part of our evening existence, and so it would have to be until we were making more power. Going around by flashlight gave us that kids-in-their-fort feeling. Carrying candles on a tray whisked us back to another century.

But reading was easier in daylight. And so was everything else. As August wound down, we got up earlier and earlier in the morning and went to sleep before nine, calling each other "o baa san" and "o jii san," "grandma" and "grandpa"; quite a switch for two Downtown denizens who used to leave for the party at ten or eleven and come home closer to three.

When we were moving in together in Downtown, I heard Shingo use the word "ambivalent" for the first time. With some of his belongings at our new loft, some at his old loft, and some at my Zen Center apartment, he couldn't find anything and couldn't get anything done.

"I ambivalent YOU," he blurted, out of nowhere. I liked it a lot: here was a man who could express his feelings.

Now, as off-grid novices, there was no time for either of us to be ambivalent. We were both too busy deciding what needed to be done next:

Buy drinking water? Chop wood? Buy fire lighter? Fill the gas can for the generator? Do we need oil? Too soon for propane, right? Is there something we forgot?

Our first month off the grid was bringing home how much we consumed in terms of energy. And water. And food. It made us grateful for any and all of it.

"But we need more frugal," said Shingo, using that other long-ago-learned word to express our growing awareness.

After a month in the country with no TV, our conversations no longer included the latest fear-mongering news from Washington, Wall Street, or the Los Angeles police blotter. They sounded more like excerpts from The Farmer's Almanac.

We talked about the weather and what it might be like tomorrow; what time the sun would be rising and setting – day length was important to us now; high and low tides; the phases of the moon; the dates of meteor showers and where it would be dark enough to see them (in the front yard if the night sky was clear).

On this island of world-renowned telescopes, Shingo even tried to teach me a little astronomy: how the earth goes around the sun, and the moon goes around the earth. Or is it the other way around? Sorry, I'll never get it.

We couldn't stop enthusing about the air, sea air, mountain air, fragrant air you could breath, so different from city smog and stench; the tastiness of locally grown fruit and vegetables and caught-this-morning fish – at Suisan, a fish store in Hilo, they put the name of the fisherman on the package.   We couldn't get over the brilliance of the moon and stars at night and in the early morning; rainbows and moon halos; the deep perfume of white ginger, suddenly in bloom; the absence of noise, except for our water pump and the **###** generator (insert five-dollar epithet of your choice).

That generator, reminiscent of jackhammers under the windows of our L. A. loft, was a heart-breaker.   At least when we turned it on we weren't disturbing anyone but ourselves and a coqui frog.

"Coqui, coqui." "Coqui, coqui."

Oh, no!   I just heard a coqui duet.

There are two of them out there.   Breeding.

I really hate to say this, but, "Neighbor, tonight you die."

SEPTEMBER IN PARADISE
Do It Yourself

We've always been Do-It-Yourselfers. The lofts we moved into were bare-bones, with tenants expected to put up walls, erect a mezzanine, put in a kitchen, tile a bathroom, install soundproofing, add laundry equipment, or whatever was necessary to make life livable. But here, off the grid in the country, it was all Do It Yourself. Though in the past I'd planted flowers and trees, which I grew from seed, on Downtown city streets, I never imagined myself repairing a road.

While waiting for furniture to arrive we decided to improve Road Nine by putting gravel in all the potholes. And why not do our muddy carport too? And why not put some at the gas-and-electric-operations side of the house where the mud was so squishy after a heavy rain it sucked at your rubber boots.

We discovered we could buy gravel of various sizes at a pit in Hilo. Three-quarter inch "base course" is what they recommended for a road. It would be loaded into our truckbed by their heavy equipment and they'd charge us by weight; so we'd go in empty, fill up, get weighed, and pay $35.00 a ton on the way out. To do this, we'd have to take the camper shell off our truck.

On "road day" we got up early to prepare, but after unscrewing the camper shell and trying to move it, we discovered how heavy a camper

46

shell is. If we laid it on the ground, we knew we'd never be able to lift it back onto the truck with just the two of us.

There was head scratching, and then . . . light bulb! Finding a pair of wooden construction sawhorses under the house, we took them out to the road. Positioning the truck in front of them, and using our backs to slightly lift the camper shell, we could slowly slide it onto the sawhorses. This set-up would allow us to get under the shell again, and use our back strength and leg strength when it came time to lift it back up onto the truck.

Having lived so many years in an industrial neighborhood, I've always been fond of heavy equipment. I'd guess there's many a female, not only me, who'd love to climb into the cab of a backhoe and turn the key, and these days there are a quite a few women who do.

Though I wasn't running it, it was good fun to go to the gravel pit and be loaded up by this dinosaur-looking machine, which swiveled and scooped and deposited as much gravel as we could carry, with a series of tremendous roars, into the back of the pick-up.

The load of gravel weighed a ton. How many times have I used that expression without knowing what a ton really looked like or felt like? Our truck could carry exactly a ton of gravel. Huh! So that's why it's called a one-ton truck.

With the weather co-operating, we started filling potholes that day at the top of our street, Shingo shovelling gravel off the truck, and me spreading it below. It was easier to spread with the side of my rubber boot than to try to use a rake or a shovel – leg strength again, and boy, was it good exercise for the inner thighs.

But one ton of gravel doesn't go very far. We'd hardly filled the potholes in a third of the road when we ran out.

Four trips to Hilo and four tons of crushed rock was the eventual tally, over the next few days, to finish the road and do our carport and the side of the house. We personally handled every pebble of four tons of gravel, and, after we were done, managed to boost the camper shell back onto the truck.

Sound sleep came very easily at night. We awakened to sore muscles, but a real feeling of accomplishment. And our Do It Yourself road repair had cost less than $200.00.

Here in the rainy rainforest, plants are exemplars of Do It Yourself. Never mind buying a rooted cutting, just chop off a piece of whatever you fancy, strip off three of its lower leaves, push that part into the ground, and it takes care of the rest. Even a rustic fence at the side of our driveway, made from branches of old dried-out guava, is growing: the fence is making leaves, can you believe it?

When pigs come rooting on the lawns, as they have been lately, if we stomp down their diggings, the grass takes over, covering muddy scars in a week or two or three. No need to re-seed or re-sod if we're willing to put up with the mess for a while.

I'm a gardening freak, but Shingo gave me a turn when he said, soon after we moved here, "I no interest plants." All I could think about was plants. Every plant I saw along the highway, every plant in any garden, was a possible candidate for our landscape, though I forced myself, with uncommon willpower, to hold back, sticking to a color scheme and a garden plan.

Now, however, seeing the ease with which they grow, and their infinite variety, Shingo has cast his artist's eye on plants. He wants to grow pale blue ones, maroon ones, giant fan-shaped ones, too-tall-and-skinny ones, plants I don't particularly like. Even if I pass them by, I see he's bringing home cuttings and putting them in places where he doesn't think I'll notice.

I don't want these plants in our garden. I don't want to look at a hodge-podge. But I don't want to stifle the urges of a budding horticulturist who's forgetting to be a city boy.

Still waiting for furniture, we decided to interview a solar contractor whose name we found in the house files, but, upon his arrival, discovered he didn't put our solar panels in, though he said he "might have" sold them to the former owner. Mr. Off The Grid, that confident Do-It-Yourselfer, apparently installed them.

And he put them in backwards! They faced North instead of South. They'd have to be turned around.

And we'd need at least four more panels, not two, and a bigger inverter, and a better voltmeter, and a charge controller, and four more batteries, plus installation materials, and labor. We were looking at more than seven thousand dollars, not the two thousand we were expecting.

But our electrical needs, as the contractor estimated them, would be taken care of. The system could be connected so Shingo would never have to use a battery charger again. And we could get a voltmeter installed indoors so we wouldn't have to go out in the rain to see how much electricity we were making and using. He would even shave the price if Shingo would help with the installation so he didn't have to hire an assistant.

We decided not to wait for the furniture and appliances. We'd go ahead. Trust again: "Yes." And Shingo would help, and, "Yes, let's do it, please. Two weeks? Sounds good!" I said, as I handed over a deposit.

With dread for our budget but with high anticipation of enough electricity, we began to count the minutes until the solar contractor would come. As it turned out, there were a lot of minutes to count.

Well, sue me. Budget to the wind, I just bought another orchid at the Farmer's Market in Volcano.

"Family price, seven dollars. You take this plant home!" insisted Meiling Okimoto. How could I say no? Even though it's the third orchid I've brought home this week.

They're practically giving them away. And not just at the farmer's markets and nurseries - they're everywhere: at the grocery store, the hardware, even the gas station.

I've tried to grow orchids more than once, but could never provide the filtered light, high humidity, pure water, and ten to fifteen degree temperature drop at night they need to thrive; conditions people emulate with growlights and greenhouses, and shadecloth and specially filtered water supplies, buying thirty-two books on orchids to learn how to do it.

Right outside our door, all that's a given. It's a medium-to-cool-growing orchid's natural habitat. You just slap them on a tree, or set them in the ground, if that's what they're used to, in the right light, and feed them once in a while, and they Do It Themselves, rewarding you with displays of color and form that'll leave you gasping.

I know an orchid has little to do with sustainability or living off the land. It's not a chicken. It isn't spinach. But isn't unfathomable beauty just as important to survival?

During our interview, the solar expert had made and received phone calls, getting perfect reception on his cellphone at our house.

"I've got four bars," he'd said.

"What's that mean?" I asked.

"It's the strength of the signal," he replied, with a look that chalked up the depth of my ignorance. "See? Here, at the top of the phone, it shows you."

I swallowed my no-tech embarrassment. Now we knew what cellphone service to buy.

Within days, we'd switched phone companies, and never again had to go out to the road in the rain to make a call, but had to buy new handsets, change our phone numbers (our calling card phone number wasn't portable), notify everyone, and program the phones.

Try explaining those confusingly complicated instructions in the manual, which you don't understand yourself, to someone who speaks "Shinglish." Top-notch teamwork on the road segued to frustration and arguments over our lifeline to the outside world.

"No, no! Don't touch that button. You'll screw everything up! Stop!"

"Why I need stop? I need call Japan!"

Men think they can push buttons until they figure things out. Women just want simpler instructions and maybe a Valium or two.

Then we had to learn to understand our calling plan, for which we needed a Masters in math and a Phd in cellphone-ese, not to mention a lesson in cause and effect: that if we went over the allotted minutes in our "family plan" we'd be paying 45 cents a minute for every call thereafter. We hadn't yet learned to make long chatty calls to our friends "across the street" on weekends, when minutes were free. Brief "We've changed our phone number" calls were turning into talk-story about feral pigs, which were making regular, earth moving, appearances; the nightly coqui frog musicales which seemed to be getting louder; the mystery of the still-missing furniture; and tales of four tons of gravel. We didn't yet know how to check on our minutes, but logic suggested that our first phone bill from the new company was going to be rude.

Exceeding-the-budget worries, though, were offset by the pleasures of the Do It Yourself garden. Just looking out any window or taking a stroll to the end of the driveway, or wandering around the backyard, turned angst into awe.

I wish I could rename the tropical plants making a distracting splash out there. Anthuriums. tillandsias. bromeliads, heliconias: there must be a better way to describe their elegance, toughness, and adaptability, or, at least, say what they look like, the way staghorn fern says staghorn fern.

Those waxy heart-shaped flowers on long straight stems, seeming almost fake they're so perfect, should have a lovelier name than "anthurium." "Valentine-on-a-stick," is close, but too sentimental, too one-note, not worthy of that majestic, ever-blooming, plant.

Tillandsias, sharing hapu'u fern tree trunks with orchids, take the spiky shapes of sea urchins, or drape down like bundles of gray/green string, or emerge from swirls of mottled leaves with cobra-heads of purple flowers, or send out wiry dark red stems ending in lime-green florets. They come in so many shapes, sizes and colors I can't come up with a name that suits them all. I just know "tillandsia" isn't it. And the same goes for their cousins, the bromeliads, whose whorls and cups produce the most intriguing lollipops and swags and starburst bracts, whenever they're in the mood.

51

I do know what I'd call a heliconia, with its colorful lobster-claw-like inflorescences curving out of shiny dark-green leaves. I'd call it "Hog Chow."

At least I would today, after pigs ate the heliconia given to us by Clayton Amemiya, whose own garden is a showplace. We planted it so lovingly, with cinders for drainage and plant food in the bottom of the hole, and have been eyeing its progress daily, dreaming of outlandish blooms. But that's never going to happen. Not a leaf, not a stump, not a root is left. Some big pig inhaled it all.

From roadworker to painter: Shingo had been urged by a long-time island resident, a friend he's known for forty years, to enter a portrait competition on Maui. While we were on hold for furniture and our new electrical system, he used our empty screened lanai as a temporary studio, where he seated his subject (the friend), took impressions and made his painting. The screened porch, about nine feet square, was not the enormous loft space he was used to working in. He didn't complain. Happy to be painting, he completed the portrait quickly, but in our damp climate the paint refused to dry. Still slightly tacky, the portrait passed the jurying process. We'd be going to Maui, all expenses paid, or so we were told (by the friend), in January.

We'd been getting to know more people and even entertaining at our makeshift dining table, though our guests tended to leave soon after dinner. Was it something we said? Was it too hard to relax without a single chair to sit in? Was it because they'd have a long dark country-road ride home? Or was it just that they they went to bed early?

We chose to believe it was the early-to-bed, early-to-rise scenario. People on The Big Island had urgent business at dawn: calling New York, sitting in meditation, going fishing, tending a garden, firing a kiln, or just enjoying the sunrise.

Hawaii-born people kidded us about living in Glenwood, the name of our area, calling it "Gloomwood" or "Graywood" or "Glenwet" but we defended the land we belonged to.

"It's not that wet!" we'd say, straining only slightly to have our voices heard over the roof-racket of a sudden downpour.

They gave us detailed advice about coqui frogs and their habits. The frogs were ventriloquists, they said. They could throw their voices, and we'd have to have keen ears and sharp eyes to find them. To hand-catch coquis, they suggested we go out after dark as a team with one person holding a flashlight and the other grabbing the frog; nevertheless we were still unable to find, much less kill one. Our unsuccessful forays turned the old saw about "How many Zen students does it take to change a lightbulb?" into an ongoing night-time joke.

As to pigs, their counsel was brutal: get a gun, or a big mean dog, neither of which we wanted.

"Pigs here long time," Shingo said, "This they territory, not us's." He wanted to co-exist.

To our complete surprise, one of our guests found an overgrown abandoned cabin on the next-door property.

"There's a roof over there," said Valerie Nakao, pointing through the jungle.

We'd never noticed, perhaps because we'd been told we had no neighbors. And that suited me fine. I pictured nude sunbathing, if we ever got a full afternoon of sun, but Shingo, that social animal, wistfully wished we had a human next door.

Exactly two days later, our erstwhile neighbor showed up, a man named Big Dave Little, quite a tall person, a musician from L. A., who was planning to move back here within a month. I told him he was a figment of Shingo's imagination.

Towards the end of the second week of September our belongings finally arrived, but the forty-foot container couldn't make it up Road Nine. Though we'd filled the potholes and the wreck had been towed, overhanging trees and no place to turn a big-rig around made Road Nine an impossible "No can!"

The island movers, totally pro, and used to this sort of thing, parked the container on the main paved road and shuttled an unending line of boxes and crates and furniture to us in smaller loads, in a smaller truck. There could have been an unsettling charge for all the extra work, but, because of the lost container and the long wait, our L. A. mover covered the contingency. Whew!

We'd carefully labelled every box, and even had a plot plan for the furniture, but as soon as things started coming through the door we knew we'd brought too much. Where to put it all? Where to put the art, a roomful of it? Our house, once so spacious we rattled around in it was now full up to the rafters.

And we were no longer "on vacation." It was back to Do It Yourself.

Our daytime routine:

Grab breakfast - no toast - not enough electricity - eat cereal.

Clean out fireplaces.

Unpack, sort it out, put it away – where?

"Shingo, can you lower the kitchen cabinets? I can't even reach the second shelf!"

Grab lunch.

"Where gone screwdriver feel its bit?"

"Huh? Oh, the Phillips? I'm using it, honey."

If sunny, open all the windows and sliding doors to let in some warmth.

Then, in liquid sunshine, run around and close them all again.

Go to dump with full truckloads of cardboard and packing paper and regular garbage.

And/or go to laundromat/grocery store or farmer's market/buy drinking water.

Go to gas station for propane/generator gas/gas for truck. Buy another orchid?

Go to post office for mail: what time do they open and close?

Go to library for internet, but not on Saturday or Sunday.

"What day is this?"

"Monday."

"I think it's Tuesday."

"I confuse."

54

"Me, too."

Weather permitting, put in time on the garden: pruning, pruning, pruning – hapu'u ferns' green fronds turn brown, droop down, look eerie: they are not low maintenance.

Get distracted by beckoning perfume of wild white ginger along the road. Pick an armful and arrange it in the house.

Until reminded that it's time to chop kindling, split wood, and stack it at the fireplaces.

I was, and still am, impressed by Shingo's karate woodchopping technique. The longhandled axe over his head, the Bruce Lee shriek, "Hiiiaaaaa," he can chop a huge log in two with a single stroke, one of many unforseen talents of the city boy.

Our nighttime schedule:

Start horrid loud generator at sundown still using battery charger.

Start living room fire.

Make dinner: don't use oven - generator will be on too long.

Set table: now we had a real one with chairs.

Dine on local chicken, pork, fish, vegetables and fruit: Shingo said he'd move to Hawaii just for the mangos.

Do dishes: our own were slowly getting unpacked.

Start bedroom fire.

Hunt coqui frogs unsuccessfully, but get extremely muddy.

Or . . . Lie down on sofas, unintentionally fall asleep.

Or . . . Take bath(s), fall asleep in tub.

Hang wet towels on new clothesline on screened lanai, where they'd take about three days to dry.

Tend fires.

View moon and stars from back steps. Compose haiku - straight out of the pages of *The Tale of Genji*, except for the quality of the poetry.

Turn off inverter.

By flashlight, go to bed, but lie awake wondering when the solar contractor would come.

"He say two weeks. Now over."

"He's wrapping up another job. He says maybe a few more days."

55

"What meaning 'wrapping'? I no like 'maybe'."

The moment gardening tools and plastic pots were unpacked, I started to plant cool-weather vegetables, hoping that they, too, would adopt a Do It Yourself lifestyle.

I'd always had a "farm" in window boxes, or in pots and baskets outside our last L. A. loft. There, in the dry, harsh climate, the harvest was a roaring success if five or six eggplants, a handful of teeny-tiny carrots, and enough lettuce for a few salads came to the table. But here it was going to be different. Here, on our own land, I'd grow overflowing bushels of produce like the proud-planter photos you see on the covers of seed catalogues.

Within days, seedlings of beans, and spinach, and peas, and lettuce, poked their heads above the soil. I could almost watch them grow from the kitchen window. But, in too much rain, they soon turned moldy, damped off, and fell over, and even the outdoor table holding the beginner pots sank, at a drunken angle, into the mud. Food self-sufficiency in rainforest Hawaii? Grow what you eat, eat what you grow? Not yet.

Slightly more successful was a compost heap started at the back of the garden in a garbage can, with 1" holes drilled all over it for aeration. This took away about 1/8th of our household waste, and the compost would be good for the vegetables, once I learned how to grow them.

Shingo, my hero in all other things, wouldn't, and still won't, go near the compost can. He's scared of what flies out when you take off the lid, and what you see inside. I don't mind clouds of fruit flies, rot, maggots and the occasional escaping rat. They're making black gold, Doing It Themselves. I like it. I'll go.

September was on its last legs by the time we got a firm date for the solar contractor to install our new electrical equipment.

We anxiously watched the weather. And we were in luck: on installation day the sun arrived. But he didn't. It was raining at his house, he said, and he "assumed" it was raining at ours.

He had a phone. Couldn't he have picked it up? I asked, as gently as possible, as he put us off again.

He was a much better salesman than he was an installer. More delay, start and stop, too many excuses, too few tools, zero design sense, using Shingo for all the heaviest work, and $7,500.00 later, he completed the job, but not before a certain Zen priest, normally a peaceful person, gave him a yell, demanding that he come on a sunny Sunday morning and finish up. We refused to wait another minute, which was sure to turn into another week.

Shingo wasn't the only one yelling. We could hear another of his clients blowing up that Sunday morning, as he held his cellphone away from his ear, with the same lame excuses – "I'm not an early riser." "I need to buy screws." - being offered to another irate customer.

After an unpleasant few hours we were connected, at last, to the sun. But then, as he was leaving, and only then, the contractor let us know we'd probably have to run the generator if we wanted to use the toaster, a vacuum, a hair dryer, the oven, or Shingo's life-support, a rice cooker.

His parting sentence, said with a chuckle, destroyed the last of our trust in him and his professionalism:

"I'm starting to get it that the only people who want solar are the ones who have to have it."

Sure we had to have it. We live off the grid. But we still expected to live like citizens of a modern country.

That hope faded as the day progressed and the sun went down.

We still didn't have much more electricity at night than we'd had before, because of the half-baked way he set us up.

He hadn't connected the new solar panels with the old, as planned, so we ended up with two separate systems, one which ran the pump for the water, and one which ran everything else.

Since the storage batteries weren't joined either, we had too much storage for the pump and not enough where we needed it most.

Nor could we, any longer, turn off the inverter before sleep to save a little energy for the morning: as he installed it, it was far away, under the house.

Did we demand that he fix things or change them or give us money back?

No.

We never wanted to lay eyes on solar-pundit again.

When thinking of him, two five-dollar Japanese expletives arose: "Manuke!" meaning "You have bad timing!" and "Baka!", even stronger, which translates as "You can't tell the difference between a deer and a horse!"

It took a lot of "Be here now" to keep from my mind a cheap, over-used American expression roughly meaning "Do It Yourself."

5

OCTOBER IN PARADISE
Fears And Smiles

Newbies off the grid, we had five underlying fears, the kind that make you subtly stressed though you might not be conciously thinking about them:

1. Fear of running out of propane: If the big tank runs out, the stove won't work, the fridge won't work, and everything in the freezer will defrost. If the smaller one runs out, there'll be no hot water.

2. Fear of running out of electricity: Can solar panels die? What if we ruin the batteries? What if the generator breaks down?

3. Fear of running out of catchment water: We won't be able to flush a toilet, wash a dish, or take a bath.

4. Fear of wood-burning stoves: Will they continue to work well or will they burn the house down?

5. Fear of cesspool: Will it get too full and back up? Eeeewww!

We ran out of propane, the first time, early in October, while cooking dinner, on a Sunday, when you'll never find a doctor or a plumber or a propane dealer open.

Mr. Off The Grid had installed a twenty-five gallon metal tank (which, I now know, weighs 180 pounds when full) to supply the stove and refrigerator, and a ten-gallon tank (weighing 80 pounds full) to supply the hot water heater. Lifting them up to hear whether liquid was sloshing around in either of them was not the most scientific way to tell how much propane was still in there.

The bigger tank was too heavy for one person to carry, whether empty or full. Two of us had to muscle it in and out of the truck, which made a propane run something to procrastinate about, especially if it was pouring rain.

On this particular Sunday evening it was the stove/fridge tank, the biggie, that had emptied, but, at first, we weren't sure what was happening.

No flame? Was there something wrong with the stove?

Uh oh! The fridge wasn't humming along either.

We must have run out of gas. A trip outside to jiggle the tank confirmed it.

"Be here now," suppressing hysteria, we scrounged around for our camping equipment: a Coleman stove and coolers, still in boxes in the carport; dug them out, cooked dinner on the Coleman, put the fridge contents into the coolers, took the opportunity to defrost the freezer - and throw snowballs - and went for propane early Monday morning.

It was good to have coped so well, but, a week later, again on a Sunday, we ran out again.

This time we had no hot water from the on-demand heater, so, of course, we heated water on the stove to do dishes, and didn't take baths that night.

But there had to be a way to make life a little easier.

With advice from two of Hilo's propane dealers, we decided to replace our twenty-five gallon fridge/stove tank with two ten gallon ones, which were a little lighter to carry, and add a five gallon tank to the ten-size we were using for hot water.

A gizmo with a fuel guage and a lever could be installed between each pair of tanks, which would let us switch over to a full tank as one

60

emptied.   Shingo would still have to haul heavy tanks around every four or five weeks, but a little fold-up handcart I picked up in Hilo would help with the chore. (I know he hates to use it, though, because it's pink.)

Whenever I think of Hilo, I have to smile. It's demanded that I do. Someone, on their own, has tacked handlettered signs, quite a few of them, to electric poles along the old highway. "SMILE!" they say. Even when I'm not there, I must obey.

When I am in Hilo, there's lots to smile about: the gas station kid who says, "Thank you, Auntie," and melts my heart. The teller at the bank, who says, playfully, "Come again!"

At the police station in Hilo, where we recently went to get our drivers' licences, I heard a teenager tell her mother she hated her photo:

"My hair's too bushy," she complained.

I said, "Show me. I'll be an impartial judge," and she handed it right over – can you imagine this happening in L. A.?

Examining the photo, I exclaimed, "You look terrific and your hair is gorgeous." - not a lie. She went away all smiles. And I was all smiles even though Shingo and I both flunked our driver's tests: I needed glasses, and he didn't study.

At the risk of saying too much about this little Hilo experience, I have to add that the teenager's mother, and two of her grandparents, had accompanied her for moral support while she applied for her first driver's license.

And that while we were all waiting for results, her mother passed out home-made chocolate chip cookies, not just to the grandparents, not just to me as I waited for Shingo, but to several other people who were sitting around.

But getting back to fears: the one about the cesspool was, perhaps, most nervewracking.

I mean, a cesspool is underground, the quantity of what's in there is unknowable. Who knew how full it was before we even moved here? Who knew which flush, which wad of toilet paper, might be one wad too many? Was it a sign of impending disgusting disaster that the grass above it was turning brown?

61

From new acquaintances with cesspools, we learned that the brown grass was a sign of a different problem, not enough earth on top of its cement cap to keep the grass alive. We could just shovel more dirt on top to give the greenery a second chance.

For our main concern, we were advised to use beneficial microbes, which we could buy in a bottle at Garden Exchange in Hilo, the store where they have everything, and know everything, about country living. We should flush the microbes down the sinks and toilets once a month to avoid the yucko event we feared. We could also use them on the compost heap.

Beneficial microbes "eat" waste and reduce the size of it quickly. Though you can't see what's in a cesspool - thank goodness - you can see what's in a compost heap. Kitchen and garden waste was noticeably reduced within a few days after sprinkling with the microbes, so something "beneficial" was hopefully going on with that other waste underground.

That first October in the rainforest, we had no fear of lack of water. Plenty fell from the sky. But so did leaves from the tall ohia trees around our house. Roof gutters, conduits for our water, needed to be cleaned.

We were also told by other catchment users to make sure there were no vermin on the roof and to eliminate obvious rat-ladders, since germs from their droppings can be a dangerous health risk if they get into the water.

We chopped down branches of trees which led to the roof, not fully understanding that a rat is a reincarnation of a Hollywood stuntman whose father was a miner and whose mother was a tight-rope walker, who, just for kicks, scaled the South face of Mt. Everest. They can gnaw through wood, plastic, even metal screening; climb a smooth vertical surface, or tiptoe along a 1/2" ledge. We'd have to keep a sharp eye out for the little black pellets that spelled "R. A. T."

We found them, soon. Not on the roof, but in the cabinet where our water heater and filters are installed. Unacceptable! There must be zero rats anywhere close to our water supply.

I hurried to a hardware store for a method of execution. Not poison: we didn't want to find dead rats rotting in unexpected places, nor would we want to unwittingly poison an owl. Not snap traps: they're inefficient, and you run the risk of demolishing your finger instead of a rodent.

At Ace Hardware, in the shopping plaza at Kea'au, I found the ideal weapon: "The Rat Zapper," a device which electrocutes the animal, supposedly humanely. I happily spent the $34.00 to bring it home – there are times when it's foolish to be frugal.

That night I caught the first rat. A red LED light blinking on The Zapper announced the kill in the morning, though a long black tail sticking out of the bright blue death chamber was enough of a hint.

Wearing rubber gloves and preparing to double-bag the critter before throwing it in the trash, I was feeling quite proud of myself, while Shingo, less bloodthirsty than I, looked the other way and accused me of murdering Mickey. I defended my reputation, dangling the biggest rat I've even seen, and chasing him around the yard with it.

Over the next seventeen nights, I zapped seventeen rats. I zapped them near the birdfeeder; next to a bag of plant food they'd invaded by the front door; on the top shelf of the tool cabinet – what did they want there and how did they get up there? - and, most often, and most importantly, inside the water-system box where they couldn't seem to get the message that the electric chair awaited.

Bagging up dead rats from hard-to-reach locations gave me new respect for rats: for their awesome feats of breaking and entering and climbing sheer vertical surfaces. Allowing them their dignity in death, I didn't examine them closely, so I never did find out exactly what Shingo's favorite Korean swear-word describes.

Then, as suddenly as they'd arrived, the rats were gone, and so was any trace of rat pucky anywhere near our water. The only reminder of their intrusion was the strong smell of disinfectant.

As Mr. Off The Grid had told us, it would take three different filters and considerable expense to make catchment water potable. It was easier and cheaper to buy drinking water, as he'd said, though Shingo had to trundle five gallon bottles back and forth between our house and a local gas station/general store. That is, until someone, in the dead of night, stole the store's entire water filtration system and dispensing machine. After that he had to drive about an hour, there and back, to Kea'au, to get it.

Still we bathed in simple filtered catchment, brushed our teeth with it, flushed with it, washed dishes in it, and used it to cook with, as long as it was boiled. Though we knew bird poop might occasionally wash into it and algae and bugs lived and died in it, and "Please no!" a rat might someday find its way to the roof, we thought of it as The Ganges.

We did have to change the main water filter whenever it was dirty. Hint: the water in the toilet looked a little green. The first time, Shingo didn't follow instructions and didn't drain the water lines. Water sprayed everywhere, but what did he care? It was raining as usual. He was already soaked.

Our woodstoves were working beautifully and were easier to run now that we had more experience.

I'd always thought a "back-log" referred to work left undone. What it really is is a big log you put in the back of your fireplace. And then you put in a front-log, with a twist of paper between the two. A blob of solid firelighter atop the paper, lit with a wooden match, creates a lasting flame to which small, then larger, kindling can be added - this is one case where size matters. Then, once some glowing red coals are happening, more logs can go on.

Learning to adjust the damper which controls the air a fire must have to succeed, finding the perfect level, meant we didn't have to spend as much time on fire duty, but we'll always have to fuss with air intake each time we add a new large log.

We were burning everything we could in order to decrease our trash, making for fewer trips to the dump. We didn't know, yet, that we shouldn't burn cardboard, magazines, beer boxes, green or wet wood because they make too much creosote which can clog a chimney.

To dispel our underlying stress, I made a chart to fill in whenever we bought propane, drinking water, and generator gas; to note when we cleaned the gutters, changed the water filters, topped up the distilled water in the batteries for the two solar systems, and added beneficial microbes to the cesspool. Checking the chart reminded us what and when we should replenish and what needed maintenance when. Being better organized, our fears lessened.

And the woodstoves worked until November.

And we didn't run out of catchment water 'til December.

And the water-pump didn't break 'til the following February.

And the generator worked 'til May.

So I'll tell those tales of panic later.

I wonder if it's the same Hilo signmaker who put one up at our local dump saying "SMILE, ENJOY LIFE." Whoever it was, they had to climb a tree to do it.

While I was dumping trash this morning, and smiling and enjoying life, a man arrived with two Chihuahuas in the cab of his truck. They had big dog ambition, barking furiously out the window at me and baring their teeth.

"I see you brought your attack Chihuahuas," I said to him, to more smiles and enjoyment.

After the dump, I stopped by the post office for mail.

Our postal address is "General Delivery" and will be for at least a year. So many newcomers are moving to Puna, it will take that long, or longer, to get a P. O. Box. Which means we have to pick up mail between 11:30 AM and 4:00 PM and stand in line to get it, rather than going to a private box and using a key any time of the day or night.

Banks and government agencies are not that fond of a General Delivery address. It doesn't fit neatly into the fields of their computers. They'd like us to have a post office box, but I'm not so sure I want one.

It's the smiles.

I'd miss going into the post office and visiting with people who greet me by name and whose names I know – Jeri, and Velda, and Donna - as I get the mail.

65

Today I got one bill.

"Thanks," I said to Donna. "For nothing!" to giggles and smiles.

On the fears front, a less-than-subliminal one was our phone bill paranoia, which turned out to be justifiable. The first bill from the new cellphone company was more than triple the expected charge. No wonder - we were using the phone instead of e-mail.

"You can get wireless internet," people had told us all along, sounding somewhat superior and in-the-know. And that's true, if there are transmission towers within radius. In L. A., I was assured by a Big Island wireless provider that new towers were going up in our neighborhood in July. But July turned into August, then September, before he apologetically admitted that his funding had dried up. No new towers. No wireless internet. "Sorry."

"You can use a cellphone as a modem for the internet," we were advised by other know-it-alls: yes, but it sounded expensive and slow. Then the capper: a wireless maven friend, passing through with his laptop and phone, said our new cellphone company wasn't the best source of this service. Another carrier was much better and faster and we should switch.

Of course, we'd need a new computer.

I put fingers in my ears. Enough rigamarole! For now, going to the library to get on line for free would be just fine.

So much for our #1 house-hunting priority, the internet at our fingertips, but somehow, we didn't miss it that much. Shingo was glad of an excuse to escape e-mail, which took him just as long to write in Japanese as it did in "Shinglish." Both of us preferred personal contact by phone where you could hear how people were feeling by the sounds of their voices, no matter what they actually said. All we needed to do to lose our fear of phone bill and enjoy the telephone was to understand our calling plan and play it like a game.

We could make long phonecalls "across the street" on weekends and after nine at night without spending the minutes in our calling plan, though we'd still have long distance charges for Canada or Japan.

"After nine PM" worked well for calls to a telephone banking system or for picking up messages, but we didn't call the mainland much after nine because of time differences, and it wasn't that useful on our island: most people were already snoring.

You don't learn to play chess, or bridge, or Go, in five minutes. So we forgave ourselves the over-budget phonebills, and resolved to learn, a little at a time, the ins and outs that would help us become masters of the cellphone game.

In the "SMILE" department, a new Hawaiian friend, Charlie Nihipali, who's helping to build a house down the road, is the number one provider of laughs, though his local accent and expressions and Shingo's "Shinglish" make for a lot of "Huh?" between the two of them.

The other day he told us about the time he went pig hunting, near here, with his brother-in-law, who claimed to know the territory. They shot one pig, but then got lost in the forest as the sun went down and a storm blew in.

Both carpenters, they couldn't make a shelter that would keep them dry. Though they cut off their pant-legs and shirtsleeves as fuel to start a fire, they couldn't keep it going. Their night was a long, wet, miserable one, shivering next to a dead pig, and wondering what their wives were thinking.

"I wanted to lock and load and shoot da kine brother-in-law," Charlie said.

If it hadn't been teeming rain, they might have heard the sounds of traffic on the highway, so close, within earshot. But it wasn't until morning, when the rain stopped, that they realized they were five minutes from the road and their waiting truck.

Ragged, hungry, dripping wet, angry, and covered in pig blood, they drove to a store to get food. When they walked into the store, Charlie said, "Everybody suck in they breath!"

When we told him we're maybe going to quit smoking, he muttered from under the hood of a car he was working on, "Maybe is da cousin of If."

It's Charlie's theory that if you make love to your wife she'll wash your underpants for a week. After that, it's "YOU wash da kine!" This is now a running gag at our house.

Charlie's cousin, Felix Ni'ihau, who likes to carve, has made us a tiki sculpture. It has a fierce face, but somehow, when I placed it in the garden surrounded by ferns, it seemed to be smiling. Even when rain darkens its brow it's still smiling. Felix just came by to see it installed, and said to it, "Keep smiling." That felt, to me, like a benediction.

Big Dave Little, our absent next-door neighbor, was not a figment of Shingo's imagination. True to his word, he arrived from L. A. and moved in towards the end of October.

Single again after a divorce, his guitar, his land, and his cabin, overgrown by jungle and leaning slightly to the right after being empty for ten years, were about all he had left – no car, no money, but somehow he was still smiling. Each morning he'd trek a few miles to the highway in the rain and hitch-hike to Hilo to find a day job, wearing a yellow slicker raincoat. He called it his "Glenwood tuxedo."

If I say musician or guitarist, that doesn't begin to cover the talents of Neighbor Dave. He could fix a computer, fix his own car, knew about electronics, did his own plumbing: having Big Dave Little next door was like getting a lifetime subscription to *Popular Mechanics* and *Wired* rolled into one.

Through Dave, we met the smiling neighbor who lived at the corner, known as Auntie Jean. She'd been there for 35 years, raised five kids off the grid, drank unfiltered water, sewed on a treadle machine, and hand-fed baby pigs.

She had a huge propane tank, which The Gas Company filled every six months. We wondered if we could get one down at our end of funky Road Nine.

Being close to the corner, she'd recently been able to get electricity and, I suddenly realized, the poles came almost halfway down our street. Feeling slightly traitorous, I called the electric company to find out what it would cost to bring electricity to our house. $5,000.00 per pole was the quote and we'd need to pay for five of them. And after that we'd have to pay for the electricity. No chuckles there.

Fears and smiles: pigs fell into both categories. It was such a kick to see a mothers and babies, but a boar could give you an aneurism. One night in late October, we saw a boar the size of a sofa at the edge of our woods. He had us quaking. But we were indoors and he wasn't, and seeing us, he wandered away.

Large or small, a pig had to eat, and, whether they came by for a banquet or a midnight snack, our lawn and garden were on the menu. It was getting to be a hassle.

I happened to own a large silver inflatable exercise ball, one of those items you impulse-buy, then never take out of the box. As pig damage worsened, I decided to try it out as a kind of scarecrow.

I blew it up and tethered it on the front lawn from a bamboo pole with light-reflecting silver plastic ribbons, hoping that the wind would blow the shiny ball and ribbons and make it look alive. But the only thing that moved it was the pigs, when they rooted all around it.

Next, I tried spreading hot cayenne powder where they were digging, but the rain washed it away before they even tasted it.

In a kind of silly desperation, I put signs on the front lawn, again adorned with flashy silver ribbons that said: "Welcome Pigs To The 354th Feral Pig Reunion." "Registration Is At Dave's" - with an arrow pointing to his place; "Dinner Is At Jean's" - with an arrow pointing to hers.

If it didn't deter the pigs, I thought we'd at least get a laugh out of it. Which we did, but the pigs weren't scared, and couldn't read, and didn't get the joke. They just kept on rooting.

The frustrating part was that we rarely saw the animals actually digging up the lawns. We'd wake up in the morning to find they'd been around the night before. Or come back from the grocery store to find they'd been here while we were gone.

If we actually saw pigs rooting, we'd run to the door and bark like big mean dogs: two full-grown adults putting all their energy and acting ability into, "WOOF! WOOF! GRRRRR!"

69

But the pigs just looked at us like "Nahhhh, that's just Lynne and Shingo," and kept on rooting.

October 31st arrived: our favorite holiday, Hallowe'en. We heard there'd be a party at the community center in Volcano, but didn't have any costumes.

At the last minute I made signs on the computer for us to wear that said "I AM INVISIBLE": not our all-out L. A. style, but they'd at least be a conversation starter.

We went the party, but it was hard to start a conversation since no one was there. Not only were we invisible, so was the party. It had happened the night before.

What could we do but smile?

6

NOVEMBER IN PARADISE
Sounds

Sounds create indelible memories, instant reminders of what you loved, and maybe, miss, about a place or time.

The roar of deisel engines on Mack trucks; the "Doom, doom, doom," of stereo sub-woofers; jackhammer racket; rapid gunfire; the thunder of helicopters; and the "Deet, deet, deet" of back-up-beepers take me back to Downtown L. A.

And we did love living there, but do I miss it? When friends "across the street" ask, "When are you coming to visit?" I say, "Never. You have to come here."

I should say, "You have to come hear."

Come and hear the ocean crashing against the towering cliffs of Kalapana or sighing on the sands of Punalu'u's Black Sand Beach.

Hear the soothing sound of rain on your umbrella.

Hear the rustle of the wind through big bamboo.

Hear the plunking of an ukulele from somewhere unseen.

Hear the night-time silence, broken only by the piercing chirp of coqui frogs:

"Coqui, coqui! Coqui, coqui! Coqui, coqui!"

Uh, strike that last part.

Hear the songbirds in our forest backyard, whose names I don't know yet, each singing its traditional melody:

"Portugese. Portugese."

"Burrito. Burrito. Burrito."

I can't tell if these birds are from Southern Europe or East L. A.

"Wheata, wheata, wheata! Would-ya? Would-ya? Would-ya?" sounds like a grain auctioneer.

Then there are sounds I wouldn't wish on anybody. Right now, dogs are baying: a pack of them, moving fast. Someone's hunting pigs. I'm worried about the little ones I've gotten to know by sight. There's high-pitched squealing and triumphant human yelling. Which little piggie will be roast pig tonight?

By November, Shingo was starting to get antsy. He had nowhere to paint. The screened porch he'd used to paint a portrait was now cluttered with things we didn't quite know where to put, and was chopped in half by a line full of hand-washing I hoped might someday dry. He didn't have the money to build the freestanding studio he wanted. What was he supposed to do? Bring his career to a screeching halt? Learn how to pick bananas?

An antsy artist is a cranky artist, an unreasonable artist. An artist with nowhere to paint is an antsy, cranky, unreasonable artist underfoot and driving me bananas.

But the answer to his problem was staring us in the face: the carport, also full of things we hadn't unpacked, already had a roof. He could build four walls and a floor, put in windows, a door, and a skylight, and he'd have a temporary studio of sixteen by sixteen feet with a ten-foot ceiling - not bad. He estimated the cost. He could do it.

Neighbor Dave, as yet unemployed, said he'd help build it. And he'd go with Shingo, to Hilo, to order all the materials.

This got me off the hook. I know next to nothing about building materials, but Dave did. Just, he was going to have to run interference for an antsy, cranky artist who imagined he was still in Japan, where building materials are perfect and standardized: no bowed lumber, no bolt that doesn't fit the nut, no tool that breaks mid-job, and the people who sell and explain it all to you do so in Japanese.

Dave was going to have to put up with the mutterings which could grow into rants about "American business," which Shingo sometimes sees as a cabal set up to personally frustrate and inconvenience him.

That, and Dave was going to have to learn "Shinglish" by the immersion method, and Shingo was going to have to learn some exotic new words:

"Shingo, we need to buy flashing."

"I no understand."

"Flashing: it's the special stuff that goes under the skylight."

"What kind stuff?"

"Uh, flashing."

I like to bake, but needing the noisy generator to run the oven had been killing it for me. Once Shingo started building the studio the generator was often in use running power tools. I'd hear that ear-splitting racket, drop what I was doing, and think, "Bake!" - run to the kitchen, plug in the oven, and toss around ingredients in a hurry. As a side effect of his building project we had cakes and cookies to eat and give away.

Notice I didn't say, "I like to iron." But if I did, I wouldn't need the generator to do it. Before leaving Los Angeles, I'd bought a butane iron, which runs on lighter fluid, mail order from Lehman's Non-Electric Catalogue.

A cordless iron: picture the possibilities - ironing in the backyard, ironing wherever you like. "Honey, let's go to the beach. I want to iron."

Though I appreciate a crisply ironed tablecloth, and a wrinkle-free pair of jeans, that butane iron, which wasn't cheap, mostly sits idle in a drawer. Here in our damp climate, wrinkles in tablecloths pretty much fall out on their own, and jeans without wrinkles say "foreigner."

Another buy from Lehman's was, and is, in continuous use in our off-grid life: an "Ecofan," made in my native country, Canada, where even city people spend summers "up North" and know something about woodburning stoves. This fan, cordless of course, and self-starting, looking somehow futuristic and old-fashioned at the same time, perches on the woodstove and runs on heat from the fire, pushing hot air into the living room.

Don't ask me how it works. Ask techie teenagers who stop by here with their parents, stare at the fan in wonder, then take it apart and go "Ahhh!"

That fan is like family, and like family ought to be: warming, comforting, quiet, and no trouble or cost to maintain. Unlike the stove it sits on, which, by mid-November, was gearing up for a tantrum and some major acting-out, which was going to cost us a lot of money.

In the distance, I can hear roosters crowing. Who says they crow at dawn? They're always crowing. They crow when the sun comes up, they crow when the sun goes down. They crow if something moves. They crow if they hear a noise. They crow for the pure joy of crowing, "I am one sexy rooster!" It's really, REALLY good that they're not next door.

"What does a rooster say?" "What does a pig say?" "What does a horse say?" In Japan, a child is taught that a pig says, "Boo boo." I told Shingo, "That's not true, a pig says 'Oink oink.'" But our Puna pigs must be studying Japanese, because grunts that sounded more like "Boo boo," came from the bushes at Dave's last night. I also have to admit that "Ko ke ko ko" is a lot closer to the truth than "Cock-a-doodle-doo."

I hear the sound of a cane toad. He lives out back in the hollow of a hapu'u root. He has a deep cello voice that sounds like Yo Yo Ma warming up. When he really gets going, "Nuh! Nuh! Nuh!" it's positively pornographic.

I don't know what sound the Hawaiian pheasant makes. A pair of them, pecking at the side of the road - he's black with a red crest and she's a dowdy brown - aren't saying a word. Perhaps when you feed on the ground and nest on the ground with mongoose and pigs and rats around, it's better to keep your mouth shut.

Shingo and Dave were sitting in the living room drinking coffee one morning towards the middle of November, discussing the building schedule. Lumber for the studio had been delivered, including beams for the floor, but they couldn't get going on it because of rain. Like two racehorses at the gate, charged up and ready to run, they waited, tensely, for a ray of sunshine to give them the starting gun, meanwhile, scribbling plans on paper in two different languages and trying to understand each other.

I thought a nice fire would cheer them, so I started one in the living room stove, adding kindling until it blazed. Then, on track with conservation philosophy - reduce, recycle, reuse - I threw in a piece of wooden construction pallet painted blue.

We'd unknowingly burned a lot of bad stuff already but that chemically treated chunk of pallet must have been the final insult. Thick smoke seeped out of the woodstove in places where smoke shouldn't be seeping. Opening the stove door to see what was wrong caused billows of it to blanket the living room and flow through the rest of the house.

While Shingo and Dave ran to open doors and windows everywhere, I grabbed a cookie sheet and fire-tongs to remove the offending fuel and rush it out to the driveway. But more trips, for a burning front-log and back-log, and red-hot coals, were called for, as smoke continued to ooze from the air intakes and the ashpan, instead of going up and out the chimney.

That woodstove was our main source of heat. We couldn't imagine a night without it, so, as the stove cooled down and the smoke cleared out, I did my best to clean it. But it soon became obvious that this was not going to be a Do It Yourself project. Strange unburned sawdust clung obstinately to interior surfaces, and had collected in places I couldn't get to. It must be clinging, and clogging, up in the chimney.

The good news? The chimney man, bless him, responding to our emergency call, arrived within hours, and returned the next day to clean both our chimneys.

The bad news? Our fireplaces were unsafe. We needed chimney collars and taller chimneys for $2,000.00 plus.

The miracle? During repairs, the weather turned sunny and warm and we didn't need the woodstoves at all: a first.

And Shingo and Dave could get on with building the studio.

I could get back to working in the garden, trying, again, to grow vegetables, understanding now that rain would be my opponent. Rain, and pigs, who'd already dug up the full-size edible mioga ginger and eggplants I'd bought at Garden Exchange and planted out in the open.

An unused dog pen at the back of the garden made from ohia poles promised security. It had a roof of clear plastic sheeting, chicken wire on all sides and a chicken wire covered door. Surrounded by trees, and backing up to untamed forest, it didn't offer the best of light conditions, but at least it would be a pig-proof, rainproof enclosure.

It took several days to weed and dig and amend the soil in the pen, but finally it was ready for planting. Cross-cultural seeds went in and were patted down in the crumbly soil: edamame, daikon, Japanese cucumber, spinach, tomatoes, lettuce.

As before, they sprouted quickly and popped up green and healthy, ready to grow and feed us. But when the plants were about 4" high we had an especially heavy rain. I watched in horror as the plastic sheeting, the roof of my "greenhouse," sagged, then filled with water, and finally broke away from its rough supports. Sploosh! It dumped a waterfall onto the vegetables, breaking or drowning most of them.

Shingo and I dropped everything to replace the roof, dodging rainshowers as we climbed ladders to staple up new plastic. But we failed to communicate about the way it should be done, and an argument began as we balanced precariously on our ladders, which got louder and louder and more personal, until we both threw down our staple guns and stomped off.

Later, I finished the roof myself, and once it was up, reseeded the damaged vegetables while sulking. But my grudge-mood soon dissipated. Digging in the dirt is a great way to get over yourself. And even a Canadian can apologize.

Again, the vegetables emerged within days and stretched for the light, but before they got four leaves, something had eaten most of them. Right down to the ground. Slugs. I found little slimy brown ones, and black/grey mottled ones the size of a pinkie finger, contentedly munching away.

Then pig-Mom and babies, unstoppable, walked right through the chicken wire, which was getting rusty, and rooted all around. They had no interest in the few seedlings that remained, just worms, fat succulent worms - "C'mon, kids! She's growing worms!" - in that fluffy soil I double-dug.

Almost four months on the land and we still hadn't grown one thing we could eat. But other people in our widening circle of friends were growing plenty. And giving it to us: bamboo shoots and taro from Russell and Valerie Nakao; oranges and avocados from Stephen Freedman; eggs and rare jaboticaba fruit from Clayton Amemiya, bananas and papayas from Paul Pang. Nobody came to our house empty handed and everyone gave us too much.

Amaury St. Gilles brought homegrown eggplant, lots of it. I'd just bought some at the farmers' market, which I hid so my thanks wouldn't seem insincere.

"I love eggplant!" I said, accepting his bounty.

"You do? I have more in the car." Shingo and I, and Dave, dined on eggplant every night for a week.

What's that sound? It must be a coqui, a new one, but he's starting to sing a cha cha, "Co-qui-qui-qui," and a samba, "co-co qui-qui." Unbelieveable: right now he's singing "co co qui qui-flat" – four bars and three notes. I've never heard of such a thing. This frog has talent. I can't kill this frog. Actually, I can't kill any frog: can't find them, can't catch them. They win.

With new neighbors and new friends we were no longer hermits, though most nights we spent alone. From L. A., we got word of the latest TV series which we might have been watching had we been there. In a former incarnation, when I'd made my living writing and producing television, I'd been fascinated by every aspect of it: the story, the casting, the editing, the production values, and the human values it did or didn't embody. But in our mountain aerie, the programming friends described seemed uninteresting, unimportant, irrelevant. It was more to the point to gaze at the moon, or a flickering fire, or each other, than a flickering TV screen.

We were glad to forego the nightly bloodbath on the news. In L. A. we'd weaned ourselves from the 11:00 PM version because it gave us nightmares.

For news of the world, I subscribed to The Economist, a weekly magazine, whose issues arrived before I'd finished the last one and which was so well, and often humorously, written that I had to read it cover to cover, even if I had no real need to know about the effect of the carry trade on international currencies or the politics of Puntland.

For local information we had the weather service by telephone, recorded by a reporter with a charming Hawaiian accent; the radio – ditto; and the Hawaii Tribune Herald whose front page had more to do with a rodeo or a hula competition.

For Japanese language news, Shingo kept up his subscription to Rafu Shimpo, an L. A. daily, which arrived at our little post office a week or even a month after the events it described had happened, but which always had pretty funny haiku.

We did own a TV set and a VCR and bought a DVD player. At the Mountain View Library we could rent films, and a few PBS series, on tape or DVD for $1.00 a week. But we couldn't seem to get them up and running. We had to ask Big Dave to help us set up the equipment, and tell us which buttons on which remotes to push and in what order: another exercise for our tech-weary brains. But we rarely had enough electricity to use the system.

Shingo spent many an evening trying to spot the pigs. He'd sit on the back stairs with a flashlight and aim it wherever he heard a noise. He'd fallen in love with them and flatly refused, when they appeared, to bark like a big mean dog. And they seemed to approve of him: once, Mama Pig let him watch her nursing her babes.

I liked seeing them, too, but didn't want them to get too comfortable at our place. Generation after generation had followed their ancestors to Auntie Jean's down at the corner, just because she'd fed them, as infants, once upon a time. We could always tell they'd arrived on our street when ditches appeared on her lawn - her cute little piglets had grown up.

Which raised a question for me: piglets, when they rooted, left divots on a lawn which could be replaced with the stamp of a foot, as on a golfcourse, but when bulldozer adults got busy there was nothing left to put back. I knew they liked worms and roots, and heliconias, but did they eat all that grass and dirt, too? If not, where did it go?

Maybe the legendary little-people of Hawaii, the Menehune, followed them around with teeny-tiny shovels and itty-bitty wheelbarrows. Or maybe the pigs had their own.

Celebrating holidays in a new place can feel a little lonely. Thanksgiving, the November feast we traditionally shared in Beverly Hills at the home of my girlfriend, she who is "boisterous," "ambivalent," and "frugal," would be going on this year without us.

Every guest would bring a dish they were famous for - corn pudding, green beans with hollandaise and toasted slivered almonds, secret-recipe yams, scalloped potatoes, home-made cranberry sauce, pumpkin and pecan pies - and their sense of humor. While the turkey was being carved, we'd go around the table saying what we were thankful for.

Shingo once said he was thankful because, "I come United States ten years ago, no friends, no money, no English."

"And you still can't speak English," quipped a guest, "and you still don't have any money. Thank God you've got a few friends!"

For our first Thanksgiving in Hawaii we gave the dinner, though it departed from tradition. No turkey – six hours in the oven, with the generator on? Are you kidding? We'd all be stone deaf. It was teriyaki chicken, steamed rice, and eggplant again, but what the heck. Dave and Shingo and I gave thanks.

It's so noisy here right now I can hardly hear myself think. The string-of-swear-words generator is blasting away and Shingo's using a chop-saw. Dave is hammering one nail after another. There's a helicopter thundering overhead, flying tourists to see Kilauea Volcano. Shades of Downtown L. A., but I'm hanging in. Any minute now it's going to pour rain and all I'll hear is "Shhhhhhhhhh."

7

DECEMBER IN PARADISE
Christmas And Crisis

Running out of water became a possibility in our fifth month off the grid. We had our water catchment tank cleaned at the beginning of December which sucked out almost half the water, a result we weren't expecting.

But we were expecting our first guests from "across the street" who'd certainly want to bathe and even flush a toilet or two.

The weather was staying so sunny and dry I had to water the garden with a hose but was afraid to give it the deep drenching it was accustomed to.

We noticed water tankers going up and down the highway, so we weren't the only ones whose catchment tanks were looking low. This must be the drought the former owner had mentioned during his run-through.

In California, a drought means a year or two without rain. In our part of Puna, where everyone without a well is on catchment, a rainless week or two can be a drought.

What must it be like for people with five kids and a washing machine, or crops that relied on water? We weren't in their position, but we had to keep a close watch on the water tank. As December of 2005 progressed, it hardly rained at all.

With Christmas coming, I ordered presents from a catalogue, which can be complicated when you don't have a street address.

Road Nine is just a temporary subdivision street name - though it's been that way for 35 years! - and there are many other Road Nines in Puna besides ours. Until Road Nine has a real name, which must be a Hawaiian word or the name of a cultural figure, agreed to by all property owners on the street, vetted and recorded at the county, we can't get a house number either.

UPS and Fedex will deliver to the door, but, without a "real address," I have to give long-winded directions:

"Take Highway 11 past the blah blah mile marker, take blah blah street to Road Nine – it's marked, but the other roads aren't, so your driver will have to count. Etcetera, etcetera, etcetera, just keep coming. You can't miss it." UPS and Fedex will keep these tedious instructions in their computers for three months, but after that I'll have to recite them all over again.

Our maiden houseguest, Carmen Zella nee Mackinlay, a favorite Downtown neighbor and co-Canadian, who will sing the national anthem *O Canada!* with me, complete with trumpet, tuba, and drum parts, if anyone so much as mentions that country, came to Hawaii from "across the street" for five days to combine our December birthdays - she was turning 30 and I was turning mumble mumble.

Shingo and I had to reveal our ugly little secret: we were running low on water, therefore bathing should be held to a minimum. P.S. neither bath nor shower would be all that comfortable.

The on-demand hot water heater which Mr. Off The Grid had installed was too small, so the shower ran hot then cold, scalding you or chilling you but hardly ever pleasing you. The bath, which Shingo likes boiled-lobster hot, could never get that way. According to a plumber, this was not the fault of Mr. Off The Grid, Mr. Do It Yourself, but of the government of the United States, which had decreed that faucets of the type he'd put in must have a regulator, one which couldn't be disabled, so as not to pose a threat of burning anyone, of any age, under any circumstances, ever. The bath took at least a half hour to fill to a level which covered your knees, at which point Shingo usually added a giant pot of water he'd boiled on the stove.

Carmen Zella, unfazed, had an ugly little secret of her own.

Because we'd been complaining to our mutual Downtown friend, Youn Woo Chaa, that we had to use the noisy generator to cook rice in our electric rice-maker, he'd kindly bought us a Korean pressure cooker we could use on top of the stove. He'd asked Carmen to bring it to Hawaii, but she left it in L. A.

This, she knew, was going make Youn Woo mad.

"He already hates me," she said. "Please, don't tell him I forgot it."

Steamed short-grain white rice is sacred to both Shingo and Youn Woo. A conversation between them about rice will include the finest points about its texture and gloss and weight and tastiness. Shingo could hardly discuss Youn Woo's gift in any meaningful way without having tried it.

"Then stall," Carmen begged, "Say the pressure cooker looks great but you haven't started using it yet."

Like most Japanese people, Shingo cannot say, "No." It's too on-the-nose, too impolite. Also, he understands the very oriental idea of "saving face." So he acquiesced.

"Thank you Youn Woo, pressure cooker. Looking great. Just, I no used yet."

When Carmen went back to Los Angeles, she mailed the pressure cooker immediately, but in the Christmas crush, it didn't get here. Shingo, having told a fib, was now trapped in it.

I heard him on the phone with Youn Woo, digging himself in deeper, making excuses, mostly based on a strong attachment to his automatic ricemaker: "I so used to my way, I didn't tried new one yet," I heard him say. And the next time: "I no understand pressure cooker," whereupon Youn Woo asked for me and gave step-by-step instructions to be written down.

Finally, I heard Shingo, who'd run out of excuses, and who's a really bad liar, tell Youn Woo he hadn't used it yet because he didn't have any rice, a "watch me try and tell a whopper" impossibility.

Youn Woo, who is just as polite as Shingo, has, to my knowledge, never called him on it.

Christmas shopping took me to Hilo (SMILE) where people have real addresses: my dentist, for instance, has one you can look up in the phone book, on Kino'ole Avenue. For my first appointment, to be combined with a stocking-stuffer run, his receptionist gave me specific directions and then elaborated:

"You can't miss it. There are lots of yellow flowers out front."

I missed it and had to double back. There are yellow flowers all over Kino'ole Avenue.

Some people can't remember or pronounce the Hawaiian street names in Hilo, so it's:

"You know where the Coast Guard Station is?"

"No."

"Well, you know where Toyota is?"

"No."

"Okay, well you know where Verna's is?"

"No."

"Okay, well, just take the highway into town, turn right where it comes to an end, and look for a big a white building across from where the ships come in. You can't miss it."

Or they can remember and pronounce the Hawaiian street names, so it's:

" Take Kanoelehua to Kalanianaole. turn right to Kauhane and . . ."

"Wait, wait, I'm trying to write this down . . ."

"Never mind, you can't miss it. Just look for a big white building across from where the ships come in."

I can miss it. I have no sense of direction. Going uphill from Hilo to our house in the mountains, going from hot to cold, feels to me, a native of Toronto, like I'm going North, but it's South. The sun rises out of the Eastern woods in our backyard and sets in the Western woods across from our front yard, but I still point in the direction of Hilo and think South.

And don't ask me to navigate by the stars as the Polynesians did when they found and refound this rock we live on in the middle of the Pacific Ocean. I'd be turning the wrong way at the intersection of Mars and a comet, and end up in Tierra del Fuego.

Four more friends from "across the street" came to stay, briefly, in December but all were gone before Christmas.

And so was our water. Almost all of it. We'd have to buy some, another learning experience.

From the tankers on the highway, we'd discovered whom to call, a water supplier in Kea'au.

Simple, right? But, not. We could only order at 8:00 AM on a Monday. They'd fill the orders, as received, throughout the week. What size truckful did we want?

We had to measure the tank and call them back to find out how much it held, around 4,500 gallons, then wait until Monday at 8:00 AM to order, when their phone line was mostly busy.

Eventually, I got through and placed the order:

"The small truckful, please. Have you any idea what day it will arrive?"

The answer was "no." It could take up to a week depending on how busy they were. We'd just have to wait our turn, and be around when the delivery truck showed up. If it rained before they delivered, we could cancel.

Fine. We'd have go with the flow, so to speak. But what if we ran out of water in the meantime? If worse came to worst, we could go to a hotel, we reasoned. But could we get in during the highest of high seasons, Christmas?

Pacing, and peeking into our water tank, didn't cause the water truck to arrive. It came of its driver's own volition the very next morning.

The Christmas presents I ordered by mail, solar powered mosquito repellers and a solar powered small-battery charger, didn't come, though I haunted the post office. And neither did Youn Woo Chaa's pressure cooker.

"No packages?"

"No packages, Lynne, sorry." Jeri, our postmistress, so sincere, seemed to be taking it personally.

Not to worry, Jeri. We didn't mind waiting. Our best Christmas present was the gift of a crazy new life on a wonderful island, which Shingo refers to as "bellybutton of the world."

Though he was busy building his studio and taking guests to beaches and the volcano, Shingo made time to introduce himself to the abbot of Taishoji Temple in Hilo, and had been invited to participate, as an assistant priest, in a number of ceremonies.

"I wish he was a real priest," the Abbot, Rev. Akita, said to me. "He should go to a monastery in Japan for two years."

"At least!" I said, getting a laugh out of the Abbot, "But who's going to chop the wood?"

Buddhists have nothing religious to do at Christmas, so I usually drag Shingo to Christian Christmas Eve services to witness their ceremonies, the familiar carols, a taste of the culture I'd grown up in.

The previous year we'd spent Christmas Eve at the new Catholic cathedral in Los Angeles, a multi-million dollar mausoleum.

This time we went to Olaa First Hawaiian Congregational, just down the highway on Hale Pule Loop, a little old wooden church, with a children's pageant, and much aloha. Their modest announcement in the local paper said: "the public is welcome." We were the only "public."

The kids in their costumes, all home-made - we especially liked "The Three Wise Guys," as Shingo calls them - the innocence of their depiction of the birth of Jesus, the carols sung to an ukulele, the outdoor fellowship afterwards, as the pastor and his wife and his small congregation talked story with us and sent us home with individual bags of home-made goodies - cookies, candies, and an apple - got me high on the Christmas spirit.

We invited Dave for a dressy Christmas dinner and an exchange of gifts. He got me a can crusher: reduce, recycle, reuse. From me, he got an IOU for a solar mosquito repeller and no turkey again.

86

Christmas is not a big deal in Japan. Year's end and New Year's Day is the special time for most people, who go to Shinto and Buddhist temples, sometimes both, to ring out the old and bring in the new, praying for an auspicious year.

New Year's cards replace the Christmas cards Westerners send, and we made ours with a photograph of us, depicting our current life: studio-builder Shingo, with a paint-roller in his hand, and me, with a plant in mine, in front of our jungle home. We spent the week between Christmas and the new year sending it off to everyone we knew, feeling the connection with "us's friends" even if they were far away.

For New Year's Eve, Shingo bought fireworks and he and Dave and I set them off at midnight. Well, it wasn't exactly midnight, we'd been yawning since nine, and Shingo had to be up early to take part in a service at Taishoji Temple.

Nagaoka, Shingo's home town, is the fireworks capital of Japan. They make fireworks that go up 3,000 feet and spread 3,000 feet, and make a bang that'll rock your world. They make Niagara Falls in fireworks off a bridge, which lasts for half an hour.

Our fireworks weren't quite that impressive. More like sparklers in terms of magnitude, and making sounds like "Pffft" and "Pop," but we still said "Ooohh," and "Ahhhh," as is required.

All over the neighborhood, in pockets of the forest, people were celebrating. Guns and fireworks were going off on other streets.

After that we didn't see a pig for months.

JANUARY IN PARADISE
Pennies From Heaven

Hawaiians have liltingly descriptive words for rain: "Pakapaka ua" is a raindrop; "Uhiwai" is mist; "No'e" is a misty rain; "Ua" is steady rain; "Ka ua loka" is a downpour; "Po ino" is a storm; "Kai a ka Hinalii" is a flood. As evocative and musical as these words are, you'd rather not become familiar with them in sequence.

January brought a drenching end to December's drought. We had five straight days of ua on the roof, the pakapaka of the ua on the roof, and the weatherman said another po ino was on its way.

After buying water at year's end, our full catchment tank now spouted a steady stream of excess ua from its overflow pipe. The book-keeper in me could not decide whether to view it as money down the drain or a bonus from the sky.

Rain didn't stop Shingo's progress on his studio. Though Neighbour Dave was now gainfully employed repairing computers in Hilo, and no longer assisting – did I hear a sigh of relief from next door? – Shingo, solo, had finished the exterior, and the interior drywall. He was now painting the walls and ceiling. And, he reported, he was right on budget.

Our overall budget was a trainwreck, we already knew that, but a January accounting for the year 2005 gave us the gory details of what bumped us off the track.

The main budget busters were the move - $3,000.00 more than planned - it costs more to move from Los Angeles to Hawaii than to China; the truck - $4,000.00 more than planned; the solar panels and equipment - $5,500.00 more than planned; and the chimney changes - $2,400.00 out of the blue.

Next came fuel. Gas and propane, with prices rising every day, were costing us a bundle, and our truck only got 16 miles to the gallon.

Then came groceries. Prices for non-food items shipped to this "outer island" were higher than L. A. We tried to be frugal, but you gotta have toilet paper.

Then there were the cellphones, with bills still cruel. Long distance charges for Canada or Japan were shocking us, we'd had such cheap long distance in L. A. And we were overusing our weekday minutes: when someone's in the hospital or hurting from a sad divorce, you can't say, "I'll get back to you on Saturday."

On the upside, the new propane tanks and switches hadn't made much of a dent because we traded in the old ones.

Truck insurance was lower than L. A. – fewer desperate people, or maybe thieves, in their wisdom, know we only get 16 mpg.

There were still capital improvements to make which we couldn't do without. Solar-genius had only sold us four batteries when he could have put in eight. We were making power we couldn't store.

On our own, we researched batteries, bought four more, plus cables, and Shingo installed them himself. He had to create a complicated diagram so his cable connections would allow the new batteries to shake hands with the rest. Nice going, city boy.

Even then we were heavily dependent on the expletive-inducing generator. Without sun, and after sunset, we always had to use it. We needed a better generator but decided to stick with the old one until we could afford the best.

Anything we accomplished was accomplished in the rain which never seemed to stop. Glenwood was living up to its naughty nick-names, "Gloomwood," "Glenwet," and "Graywood." It was the same throughout the islands. No one was any drier.

But some of them were warmer. Rain fell as snow on Mauna Kea Mountain, which chilled the air at our place in the mornings down to 52 degrees. Inside. That's "Let's not get out of bed - ever" cold, "Don't hog the blankets" cold, "Wish I had some gloves" cold, "Who's going to start the fire?" cold, "Not me!" cold.

As people who belonged to the land, we had to restrain ourselves from wishing we lived at a slightly lower elevation. Just 15 or 20 minutes down the highway it was 5 and then 10 degrees warmer.

We had to remind ourselves that cold weather meant not as many bugs, though we noticed that quite a few varieties of spiders had decided to move indoors with us.

Our brand new chimney collars started leaking in the rain and needed buckets under them to catch the sudden indoor downpours. But I'm an old hand at this: every loft we ever lived in had a leaking roof. Tip from the top: put rags in the buckets so water doesn't bounce out. The chimney leaks eventually stopped on their own, I don't know why.

Our front lawn flooded and Road Nine was under water in places. Shingo made Noah jokes as if our house, like the Ark, was going to float away. He wanted to take a pair of Jackson's chameleons on board, and our two coqui frogs, though I reminded him they're both guys.

Of great concern to me was the effect of never-ending wet weather on my hair, a subject not taken at all seriously by my mate, a priest with a shaven head, who doesn't ever have to think about such things. My hair's naturally curly and in constant humidity will quickly assume the shape and texture of a Brillo pad devolving into a mat of cotton candy. I can't claim to have the brain of Albert Einstein, just the hair.

On the balance sheet for 2005, our income total was smaller than it had been. One consequence of not having the internet at home was that it was harder to play the stock market. I'd scaled down or opted out for the time being, though in past years it had provided about 1/6th of my income.

I did make some unexpected pennies because of the internet: $6.43 in royalties for an R & B song co-written many years ago called "Take Me Where You Took Me Last Night" recorded by Genie Brown, which is now somehow available again in the ether. Other old songs of mine performed by the great Ray Charles, Betty Everett, Irma Thomas, The Whispers, and David "Fathead" Newman, are out there too, earning a nickel here and a dime there.

I made $2.02 from DVDs of *The Bob Newhart Show* sold over the internet, and hear that *The Love Boat* series will be coming out on DVD in 2008. Oh boy! I'm going to be rich!

Though there's very little money in it for the writer, there's a new shot at immortality being offered by leap-frogging technologies, a new lease on life for music and film and the written word. I just hope what's out there isn't embarrassing – I can't remember the lyrics to "Take Me Where You Took Me Last Night."

In 2005 we had earned about $400.00 from our yard sale at $1.00 to $3.00 a pop, which wasn't unusual. In L. A., I'd have a yard sale at least once a year, clean out the drawers and closets, get rid of clutter, and put the proceeds toward things we'd actually use: easy to do in Downtown, just set up a table on the street.

Here, a table on the street would only attract pigs and a few pheasants, with maybe the odd cardinal stopping by to browse, and everything on it would get soaked in the ongoing po inos. There'd be no income from a yard sale in 2006.

We did have a like-new kitchen to sell, sitting useless in the mother-in-law suite, which we could advertise in the paper. And a solar inverter which we'd replaced with a better one. But de-installing the kitchen had to wait until Shingo finished his studio.

I wondered why he was slowing down, not buying the underpad and inexpensive commercial carpet he wanted for the floor, when he suddenly announced he was out of money.

Shingo Honda CPA: his idea of a budget is to get some money and spend it until you don't have any more. But he never seems to worry about it, even when his bank account is flashing warning lights.

Somehow, when he needs money, it appears. The day he declared he couldn't finish the studio, a painting sold in San Francisco.

And he had his first art show in the islands, the Schaefer Portrait Challenge, in Kahului, at the Maui Arts & Cultural Center.

We flew to Maui for the weekend, escaped the rain, met some interesting artists, enjoyed the well-attended opening night of the show, and the Hawaii-style hospitality of the Maui Arts Center staff, who covered every participant with leis. We had a good time. But only a few paintings sold, none of them Shingo's, and only the Grand Prize winner got his expenses paid.

If this sounds like sour grapes to you, they're my sour grapes, not Shingo's. He's an artist to the bone, and a Zen priest to boot. He wants to show his work, which expresses themes he cares about. To him that's more important than whether it sells. If it does, he views it as a way to finance the making of more art. If not, he'll be making it anyway, as he has during all his adult life, rich or poor, through thick and thin.

On a gray morning towards the end of January, Shingo was staring out our living room window at the continuing ka ua loka when I heard him say, "Thank you rain."

Maybe this was his Zen way of getting through soggy day after sodden night, but I know there's deeper meaning. If it weren't for rain there'd be no Shingo.

When he was two years old, his home town, Nagaoka, was the primary target for the atomic bomb because there was an important munitions factory there. It was also the hometown of Admiral Yamamoto, the Japanese commander of the war in the Pacific.

But as the crew of The Enola Gay flew over, they couldn't see their target in the rain. They flew on to a second target, Sendai, but it was the same story. Only Hiroshima wasn't socked in.

FEBRUARY IN PARADISE
Life And Death

Shingo's new studio had displaced the generator, which used to live in the carport. It was now squatting under a plastic cover outside in the rain. To me it looked angry, aggressive, no longer the pitiable aging chorus-girl, more like a pit bulldog, robbed of its doghouse, waiting for a chance to take revenge for all the curses I'd showered on it: just my imagination, and meaningless since I was rarely the one who had to work with it.

But at the beginning of February, Shingo was called away to Japan, in a rush, because his next-eldest brother - the one who used to fight for him when he was little, the one who dutifully stayed behind in Nagaoka to run the family restaurant, not heading off to seek his fortune elsewhere, like Shingo and his other siblings - died.

Shingo would be gone for two weeks to be with his family. I'd stay behind, giving him freedom to travel Japanese-style, fast; and sleep, in Tokyo, then Nagaoka, wherever there was room for him.

Making the saddest of plane reservations, I was torn between sympathy for him and abject fear for my own survival. It would be the first time I'd been alone for more than a few hours in the middle of the jungle, miles from civilization, off the grid, with all its challenges.

"Be here now," I had to remind myself, over and over. "You can do this. You'll be fine."

How could I doubt it? If I needed help, Dave was next door, except in the daytime when he went to work. Charlie, his wife Gina, and cousin Felix were down the road building a house. Other friends were a phone call away.

And here in Puna, even strangers treat you like their own.

Have I ever been to the dump without someone offering to give me a hand?

At the grocery store they leave the cash register to help you find the cheesecloth!

Still, I was nervous, but I put on a confident face: no need to add worry to Shingo's suddenly full schedule and deep sorrow over his brother's death.

In recent years, both of us have been having to face death more often.

Two of the most important figures in our lives, his Zen teacher and mine have both died, those inspiring elders who inadvertently brought us together.

I can't say we "miss" them: their words ring in our ears. And we often apologize aloud to them, for taking so long to understand what they were trying to instill.

What still confuses and amuses us is that they couldn't stand each other. They'd had a Zen quarrel going on since the days when my teacher, Maezumi Roshi, as a young priest, left the temple run by Shingo's teacher, Yamashita Roshi, going off to start his own place and establish a more monastic style of practice. Their animosity towards each other was, perhaps, based on a difference in mission.

Yamashita Roshi, who had been an internee during WWII, served Japanese-Americans of his era, and their families, in a church-like setting at Zenshuji Temple, with pews, and sermons, and weddings, and funerals, and memorial services, with priests imported from Japan.

Maezumi Roshi founded a residential Zen training center, Zen Center Of Los Angeles, which mostly attracted young Westerners, where you could be a monk for a minute, or a lifetime, where students in black robes sat on black cushions in meditation in a zendo, and took part in spartan retreats; and lay people, both men and women, held service positions traditionally reserved for ordained males.

Yamashita Roshi viewed Maezumi as a scandalous rebel and was viewed in turn as the priestly version of a "salary-man."

Coming from feuding Zen families, Shingo and I referred to ourselves as "Romeo and Juliet - a BIT older." We tried to reconcile our teachers, but it was never to be.

Once, I confronted Maezumi Roshi about the Buddhist precept "Do Not Be Angry" and its possible application to Rev. Yamashita. "Too much water under bridge," was all he said.

Rev. Yamashita was charming with me, and let it be known that he approved of our relationship: "Honda-kuhn has met his best partner," he told another priest, knowing it would get back to us. Maezumi, for his part, was cordial enough to Shingo, but if asking about him, would say, "How's what-his-name?"

Shingo's teacher was much older than mine, so it came as a shock that Maezumi Roshi died first. Then Rev. Yamashita went into the hospital. We were afraid we'd lose him, too.

Sensing that there might be some of the old competition involved, or that Yamashita might have even loved and been disappointed by a surrogate son, I suggested that Shingo go to the hospital and tell him, "Get out of that bed, there are other people to hate!"

I don't know if he actually said it. He claims he did, but it would be very un-Japanese. Whatever was said or left unsaid, Yamashita Roshi did get up, and was soon back performing his duties as Soto Zen Bishop of North America. He lived to be eighty-seven before joining Maezumi in that big wrestling ring in Nirvana.

As we moved to Hawaii we lost another mentor, Alec Takagi, at the age of ninety-five. Half British, half Japanese, he'd survived world war and world peace, spoke both our languages, and was our favorite model of how to live simply, and simply live to a great old age.

Having been a prisoner of war in Siberia during WWII, he couldn't bring himself to waste even a morsel of food, and would keep the smallest leftovers in the refrigerator until they were used. When we notice some past-the-due-date item in our own fridge, we refer to it as "Alec food," which means it's about time to throw it away.

Never idle, even at his advanced age, if he couldn't cook barbequed squid for the Zenshuji Temple Obon Carnival, standing over a blazing hibachi in 100 degree July heat, Takagi-san would sit to one side and chop it up for the customers. If he got too tired to chop anymore, he'd put it in take-out boxes.

He was always contributing, teaching stick-to-it-iveness and kindness by example, even teaching how to leave life behind with aplomb and grace, singing at least ten verses of a slightly off-color Japanese song in his hospital bed, at Shingo's prompting, at our last meeting.

The deaths of Shingo's elderly parents, also role models, are still fresh for us.

His father, Masato-san, said he wanted to see the year 2000, and did; then that was enough for him.

His mother, Uta-san, when told she didn't have long to live, would say, "Well, I'm supposed to be dying, but it's too hot – none of my friends will come to the funeral." Or, "I'm supposed to be dying, but there's an election on. I have to make phone calls." She lived many years past the doctors' estimate, and put on an art show the year before she passed away.

But now that his brother has died, it's the next generation going. We're members of that next generation and don't think for a moment it doesn't cross our minds.

Before Shingo left for Japan, I said to him, "Don't die."

But he replied, as he always does, "I have to."

"Okay, okay, but not now and not soon."

"We don't know," he said, matter-of-factly.

After taking him to the airport, I made my lonesome way home, not yet into the rhythm of being on my own.

With the short days and long nights of February, it was already pitch-dark and pouring rain when I went out to start the generator. I took its plastic cover off and hoped for success, but it's hard to hold an umbrella and a flashlight and start a generator with a pull-cord.

First try: I flooded it and had to wait awhile to take another shot. [Replace plastic cover so vengeful generator doesn't get soaked; park umbrella; rubber boots off; go indoors; stew.]

I gave it a second try: [Rubber boots on, umbrella up, plastic cover off.] The awful thing still didn't start, though I pulled the cord more than once with gusto, then realized I hadn't turn it ON. [Bend over, reach around to turn on machine, keeping it covered with umbrella, now getting soaked myself; push choke lever; yank cord.

Eureka! It started. [Push choke lever to "run". Park umbrella, rubber boots off, go indoors, happily await power.] But power didn't come.

The voltmeter in my office was staying exactly where it was, 24.4 - low. There must be a fault in the electric line from the generator, which was running full blast, to the batteries it was supposed to be filling. [Hole in pit of stomach – whom to call, what to do?]

But then . . . what if it was something easy, like the plug fell out when I was violently yanking the starter cord?

I went to investigate: [Rubber boots on, umbrella unfurled, flashlight in hand, glasses on face] and peered at the plug, which had YES! fallen out.

I pushed it back in. [Stash umbrella, rubber boots off, go indoors, check power – now surging! Pour a tall glass of ice cold beer, towel-dry hair, but do not sit on anything upholstered because wet clothes leave marks. And don't change clothes yet, must go out again, later, to turn generator off.]

For the two weeks Shingo was gone I hauled the wood, made the fires, dealt with the generator, changed the water filter, switched the propane tanks, changed drinking water bottles, went to the dump, not infrequently singing the theme from Rocky and flexing my arm muscles in the mirror.

Of course, I never had to actually carry, load, unload, fill, carry, load, unload and carry, any propane tanks or five gallon drinking water bottles. All that had been done before he left. I began to fully appreciate that he was Rocky with the muscles, not me. And he'd better not die any time soon, whether he "had to" or not.

For years, he and I have had a running argument over which of us should die first.

As a part-time priest in Los Angeles, and now in Hawaii, he's visited so many sick-beds and assisted at so many funerals, he claims he doesn't want to live past 75. I say he's likely to: his father lived to 95 and his mother to 88.

He says I have to live longer than him. I say I don't want to have to deal with the mountain of art he's going to leave behind.

But this is all banter. I can't imagine my life without him, whether he carries propane tanks or not. I'll be crying in a minute if I don't stop thinking about it

One morning while he was in Japan, I was working on the first chapters of the book you're reading at 6:00 AM, using the computer in the dark, knowing I didn't have enough electricity for a separate light bulb.

About 6:05 the computer quit. No lights worked either. The voltmeter, by flashlight, said 22.5 - way too low. I was afraid I might have blown out the whole electrical system and broken the only working computer in the house.

It was too early to turn the generator on and terrify Dave out of a sound sleep, so I waited well over an hour, stressing, then went to his house and called his name:

"Dave? Daaaave!" No answer. He'd left for his job in Hilo - on foot, and with his thumb out, he didn't have a car yet.

I yanked away at the generator until it started, and rushed into the house to see its effect.

Can a Buddhist say Hallelujah? This one did, as the lights and computer returned to robust good health. But there was no Rocky pantomime this time. It was back to bed for awhile, with tossing and turning, and restless dreams of a gray and white cat skulking around our bird feeder.

This was no dreamed-up cat: it was real, a regular visitor, and a menace to the birds. I'd tried to shoo it, but, like the pigs, it paid no attention, just went on about the hunting business. One recent afternoon, I'd gone outside to find it eating something. A skink? Okay. A rat? Good job. A bird or chameleon? Quit it!

"But why make these distinctions?" I asked myself. "It's all nature. Who am I to pick and choose who lives or dies?"

Suddenly, the cat shot up the tree with the bird feeder in it, in a blur of gray/white fur. The savage speed, the clawing brutality of it was chilling. But it slunk back down with no prey in its mouth. And I was unreasonably glad.

Shingo returned from Japan so tired and heavyhearted that I didn't want to bother him with little things, but the handle on the toilet wasn't returning to its "off" position, and water kept running. I could hear the pump stopping and starting, so I'd go and manually return the handle. I told Shingo this was something we'd have to do every time we flushed until we fixed the toilet, but he had too much on his mind and forgot.

I've never lost a sister or brother. I don't have any. I'll never exactly know the pain that Shingo was feeling.

But I could cry if he was crying. And I could sit and listen as he talked about his brother's life:

About the time, as a teenager, when he bought the complete Jean Paul Belmondo yachting outfit, with the striped boat-necked jersey, white pants, and a cap with an anchor on it, and wore it to the movies in landlocked Nagaoka. About how he continued in his father's footsteps making French food at their locally famous restaurant, as familiar with veloute sauce as soy sauce. About how he was known in his part of town as "King Of The Night" for his good humor and drinking habits when he unwound after a long day at the restaurant.

I tried to listen with no opinion, without wanting to fix anything, didn't push one word of Zen, just tried to love him enough to let him work through what seemed to him an unnecessary and untimely death at his own pace.

We needed some distraction, and, hoping to find rays of sunshine beyond the gloomy skies of our physical and emotional environment, went holo-holo for the day, travelling around the island with no fixed purpose and no destination in mind, stopping at a black sand beach to dawdle and dip our toes in the turquoise ocean and watch turtles surfing white-bearded breaks; riding down a stretch of highway where trees that might have welcomed King Kamehameha touched their branches overhead in a mango high-five; pausing at a favorite seaside spot, where pine needles made a dense carpet on lava cliffs and the ocean sent spumes of glistening salt water into the air, to sit around in the sun, eat ham sandwiches, and bake ourselves a new mood; visiting with fisherman angling off craggy cliffs, their rigs attached to inflated black plastic garbage bags which, blown by an offshore wind, would carry their lines and baited hooks out to sea and "catch da beeg one."

Then, somehow back on topic, we stopped at an overgrown Buddhist graveyard. The names we could still make out on the tombstones were Japanese. Some tombstones were so old the writing was illegible. Some stones, for very poor people, were just ordinary rocks which may never have had writing on them. Shingo's home prefecture, Niigata, sent many waves of early sugar cane workers to Hawaii Island: folks in this graveyard might have known his ancestors. Or been his ancestors. He was quite sure that his ancestors were the ones with no writing.

When we came back home, again on topic, the water pump had died. Too late in the day to do anything about it, we filled buckets from the catchment tank by hand and brought them in for toilet flushing and dish washing, and the next day went to Hilo for a new pump. Were we going to need a plumber too? That could mean days, even weeks without running water, so Shingo installed the pump himself, exactly copying every detail of the installation of the original. And it worked.

It wasn't until the new pump had been on duty for a few hours that we understood what caused the old one to burn out. It was the running toilet. While we were gone all day holo-holo, the toilet kept running, and the pump kept going on and off until it fried.

I lifted the lid off the toilet. Shingo shortened the chain to the ball. Problem solved.

After installing the new pump, Shingo decided he couldn't stand the volume of sound it was making, and tacked egg-carton halves - recycle/reuse - on the inside of the pump cabinet as soundproofing. It looked slapdash, but helped somewhat. Now all we heard was a repetitive groaning when the pump went on - a second cellist to compete with the cane toad in the backyard.

He then decided to build a soundproof cabinet, a sturdy doghouse for the generator. We hoped it would be less belligerent there. We'd be less belligerent towards it, if its bark were muffled.

Someone we knew suggested he use pallets stuffed with newspaper for the frame, which he did, before adding other insulation inside, and wood to match the house outside. But all the soundproofing in the world couldn't keep that mean dog quiet, and it was harder than ever to yank its pull cord.

When you're grieving it helps to keep busy. Shingo landscaped all around his studio and built a pond, where he planned to grow lotus.

He dug the lotus pond in one day, sweating and straining, covered with mud. He made channels lined with rocks for the inflow and egress of water, which, in our rainy climate, naturally collects and sometimes overflows at his pond site.

Using ohia logs from the woodpile, he built neat pathways to the pond, lined it with a plastic liner, then scouted the woods for moss and rocks and ferns and native bamboo orchids, arranging them to make it look as though the pond had always been there.

He even went shopping – a thing he avoids unless the store sells art supplies or wears an orange Home Depot sign - for a plant: a spathiphyllum, with long-lasting flame shaped flowers of pure white, and planted it next to an gnarled moss-covered hapu'u log.

On a rise by the lotus pond, he placed a black ceramic sculpture by Stephen Freedman, which looked like a pillar of lava from the Goddess Pele thrusting out of the earth.

The result was enchanting, and more than I'd expected from a non-horticultural city boy. But why was I surprised that a Japanese artist, and Zen priest, would be a natural at landscaping?

He only learned, later, from hard experience that lotus can't live in his pond. It doesn't get enough light. It dies: things change; Be here now; try water lettuce.

We were sitting on the back stairs enjoying a rare blue-sky afternoon as February came to a close, when something fell out of a tall ohia tree. A Jackson's chameleon had missed its footing and it fell thirty feet to the ground. It was stunned but alive when Shingo picked it up.

He held it in his hand for a while until it started crawling, then put it in a soft bed of moss on a tree-trunk at the side of the yard.

We kept making separate trips to see how it was doing. Not well: it wasn't moving.

Then, as I watched, it left this life. It opened its mouth and sighed, deeply, as all the air went out of its body.

As its bright green color turned to black, Shingo tried to tell himself it wasn't dead, just being a chameleon. But when reality set in, as it was finally setting in about his brother, he wanted to bury it. I wanted to leave it where it was and let it go back to the forest. I said I wished that humans could do that too, but we agreed we're just too big and smelly.

10

MARCH IN PARADISE
Mold

After two months of not your liquid sunshine, not your pennies from heaven, not your pakapaka ua, just constant pouring rainforest rain, everything in our house was going moldy. And I mean everything. You couldn't turn a corner or open a drawer without a whiff of mold.

I was on every-day mold patrol, buying every known anti-damp, anti-mildew, anti-mold concoction: sprays, powders, crystals, bleach. Some of them worked on some things, but nothing was almighty.

Anything black went moldy, with navy running a close second: here, we're talking about most of my favorite clothes. After drycleaning, and after seeing the bill, most dark clothing got donated to a recycling center. If it required drycleaning, it was history.

Anything leather went moldy: shoes, Shingo's leather jacket, my leather pants, belts. These, I cleaned with mold-killing spray, hoping it didn't also kill the leather, and put them in jumbo Ziploc bags. If the method worked we'd be able to use them again, if not they'd have to go, too.

Baskets were going moldy. I'd brought a collection of them from Los Angeles thinking how well they'd suit our new life on the land.

There'd be baskets full of fruit, baskets full of vegetables, cornucopias of plenty - not cornucopias of mold. These I washed and sprayed and spread around the fireplace at night.

Bamboo went moldy. C'mon! This is the universal material for building, decorating, and household goods, from roof beams to chopsticks, in the tropics. How dare bamboo go moldy?

I tried wiping it or soaking it in mild bleach water, which worked, but only temporarily. The next step would be to coat it with acrylic spray: a lot of work, and a lot of space, which we didn't have, for the drying.

I had to weed again, discarding a bamboo incense box, place-mats, and a pan-flute, which nobody we knew could play anyway; keeping the pickle dishes Youn Woo made, the spiral bamboo Thai serving tray, and the ikebana holders from Kamakura.

Wooden things went moldy: my rolling pin, my wooden bowls, the chopping board. I tried the bleach routine again, hoping for the best. But our entire house is made of wood!

With Shingo's studio and landscaping finished we held an opening party. Twenty people were invited and they came.

After eight months on Hawaii Island, I knew this required effort. It meant you had to change out of your muddy gardening duds, or your painting pants, or your clay spattered outfit and set aside work you loved; or cancel plans to go fishing or to the beach; or tear yourself away from a ballgame on TV on which you had money riding. You had to get in your truck, and travel a long distance just to sit around and eat and talk. Not drink, there wasn't much of that because you had to get back in your truck and drive a long distance to get home. DJ's? Dancing? Not at 2:00 in the afternoon.

If we invited twenty people and they came, and stayed 'til 6:00 o'clock, it was probably fair to say we'd made some friends. And they reciprocated with invitations to their events and favorite haunts: Stephen Freedman's art gallery openings; Professor Tzu Lung Chang's lecture and workshop on monolithic stone sculpture; Clayton Amemiya's anagama kiln firing; black history night at the East Hawaii

Culture Center; Paul Pang's girlfriend Dorothy's arrival-from-Oakland dinner; Shizuno Nasu's drop-dead-fabulous dance performances; reggae music in a field; drumming at Kehena Beach.

We had friends and we had pigs: a monolithic boar and a new mother with babies. Evidently they'd been vacationing down at Clayton Amemiya's place in the hills above Hilo since January and were coming back to see if we had any more fireworks.

At the party, he described their appetite for the rare plants in his extraordinary garden, though the destruction they left behind was nothing compared to the damage done by cows, which often breached a fence between him and a neighbor and either ate or stomped everything in sight. Even after he shored up the fence, the cows would escape elsewhere and wander up his driveway to dine and destroy.

Fences and neighbors got Stephen Freedman talking about an ex-neighbor of his who'd had hunting dogs tied up in doghouses, barking incessantly. With three acres of property, the man kept the dogs far away from his own house so they didn't keep him awake at night. Instead, he put them opposite Stephen Freedman's bedroom window. Then the guy bought 50 roosters and again put them at the edge of his property line, right next to Stephen's.

Stephen had lived and created internationally-known art in Los Angeles, maintaining a ceramic sculpture studio in Downtown: deep Downtown, South Central, home of riots and gang-bangers with machine-guns. He'd moved to Hawaii fourteen years ago to build his vision of Eden, with a rambling studio, a roomy house, acres of botanical garden, and his invitational art gallery *"idspace"*. But as he put it:

"Everyone comes here with their own idea of paradise, and if Hawaii doesn't match the dream, they get all worked up about it." After many a confrontation with his neighbor about the noise, to no effect, he realized that hunting dogs and fighting cocks were part of his neighbor's dream.

"From the land of Uzi, I get to live here," he said. "I decided to let it go."

105

There's more to the story, but I'll cut to end, where the neighbor moves away, and relatives who are more considerate move in and move the animals. But he still has to live next to noise.

We had no cows, no barking dogs, and no rooster mayhem, but the pigs were doing their I-can-dig-it damage and were even having sleepovers at our place: one night a young mother with piglets slept in our covered woodpile, first moving heavy logs around to make things more comfortable.

Shingo, suddenly defensive about his new garden and pond, had been having a change of heart about pigs - "he ambivalent" we might say - so the two of us came up with a tactic.

We camped in the backyard in our big blue tent overnight, planning to scare them. But they didn't come.

The next night we camped in his new studio with the same idea. They didn't come.

But they did come back the next night and rooted all over the place.

We were so tired from all the stupid camping; the stupid sticking flashlights in our mouths and shining them up our noses to demonstrate how we'd panic pigs; all the stupid giggling and waking each other up over every imaginary noise; that we slept right through the snorting and snuffling, the "Ack, ack," and the "Boo boo," when the pigs finally did show up.

They didn't touch his garden, though, except for nibbling a low row of dark purple hedge plants given to him by Clayton Amemiya. In some cases, where they rooted we were planning to plant anyway: the pigs actually helped by loosening the soil – or were we rationalizing? Our guests suggested this was something like Patty Hearst syndrome: when you have absolutely no control, you tend to side with your captors.

More than one guest at the party observed that the outside of our house was going moldy.

This wasn't a criticism, it's a problem for everyone on the wet side of the island, and it's not as though we hadn't noticed. The golden natural wood color we'd started out with was turning a mottled dark brown and, if you looked at the siding sideways, you could see it was fuzzy. We'd tried every product recommended by experts but nothing really worked, so we decided to call it "weathering."

We're going to have to do something, though. Maybe paint the house the color of mold. I mean it.

Shingo's paintings, too, had started to go moldy. On the backs, the canvasses were getting colorful. He joked that the backs look better than the fronts, but this was no joke. He rubbed them down with alchohol, then sealed the backs with white paint, eliminating the invitation to mold of raw canvas.

My bookshelves were going moldy. I wiped them down with a mild bleach solution. But the books started to go moldy. What on earth could I do? I donated some I could live without to the library and a recycling center. But for must-haves, I guess I'll just have to live with their mustiness.

I even found glass going moldy. Maybe it was a sign from the God of Mildew that it was time to wash some windows.

The weather stayed too wet to bring our tent in from the backyard. It was out there over a week before it was dry enough to fold up. Likewise, hand laundry refused to dry on the screened lanai and had to be brought in by the woodstove.

Shingo liked the look of clothes drying by the fire. It reminded him of his mother drying clothes that way. Until he was 12, when she got her first wringer-washer, she, and other women of her town, did their washing at the river, and carried the wet laundry back to their homes.

If that sounds primitive, remember it was post-war Japan, and that Nagaoka, though spared the Enola Gay, was flattened and burned by B29s dropping incendiary bombs.

Shingo's mother raised five kids doing hard labor until modern life arrived. And she still had to dry clothes by the fire in wet or snowy weather.

For us, modern life was receding but we seemed to be taking it in stride.

With our original woodpile running low, we cut up dead trees from the property and made a new one, hoping the wood would dry soon enough to use it. If not we'd have to buy firewood, a thing so anti-self-sufficiency we couldn't bring ourselves to do it. Talk about carrying coals to Newcastle: we live in a forest.

But we were burning a fire at night and often made one in the morning. Some days it was so chilly and damp we burned a fire all day long. After one or two nights in which water and sap could be seen bubbling on newly cut logs, an absolute no-no for the woodstoves and the chimneys, we gave up and placed an order for a cord of bone-dry ohia chopped to fireplace size. (Shhh! Don't tell Rev. Akita that Shingo doesn't have to chop wood. He'll want to send him to a monastery.)

The most annoying and unbeatable moldy smell kept recurring around our bed, a Japanese-style arrangement of a futon on tatami mats, with the addition of a foam rubber mattress for a Canadian who's used to something softer.

The tatamis were the obvious culprit. Handmade of straw in Japan, and old, they came to us from Zenshuji Temple in L. A., and had been with us in every loft we'd lived in. We'd probably brought global gobs of mold here with us in those tatamis. But we were attached to them; we loved their history; we liked the look of them and didn't want to part with them.

Shingo made a slatted base to lift them off the carpet, and often ripped the bed apart to air them as is done in Japan. I sprayed them with mildew chasers and blew them dry with a hairdryer, of course necessitating the use of the barking generator. He took them outdoors at any sign of sun, but would have to rush them back in if rain came drizzling. And tatami mats aren't light: you can't flip them around. It takes two people, with back strain, to get them where they're going.

I don't know which of us came up with the idea, I just know that it was a rare sunny afternoon, and a fellow Zen student, musician, and friend, who lives in a dryer micro-climate, was visiting.

"Would you have any use for two antique tatami mats?" I asked him.

In a Hilo minute, the offending, but beloved, tatamis were out the door, hoisted by the three of us to the top of Unzan Pfennig's van, and driven to his house where they now adorn his private zendo, and where they have not emitted a sniff of mold or mildew since.

This is still not completely true of our bed.

A few hours after Unzan left, another storm came in.

And then another.

And another.

We'd moved to Hawaii just in time for the 100 year record rains.

11

APRIL IN PARADISE
Rules

We have a rule around here: that there be no pressure. "Have to" must equal "Want to." There's always a lot of work to be done but if you've gotta do it "Right Now! Hurry Up! Go, Go, Go!" it can be a drag.

Sure, in an emergency we both hop to it. But if, on an ordinary day, Shingo wants to read, and that's all, I don't stand over him with a list.

If one of us is killing ourselves with heavy work and the other is taking a nap, nobody feels guilty.

This morning, I'm writing, he's painting: there are breakfast dishes in the sink, no wood by the fireplaces, and a streak of mold on the shower curtain; the windows need cleaning, beneficial microbes are waiting to be poured down the drains, a full day of jungle pruning is overdue, and the truck needs an oil change. These things will get taken care of when the time is right.

We have no rules about food, except to make sure to note what we're running out of on a list on the refrigerator door: this can be an interesting puzzle when "ham" is written in "Shinglish" as "hamu" and "mayonnaise" is written in Japanese.

Coming from two different cultures, we eat different breakfasts and lunches and make them ourselves.

I like peanut butter in the morning, he doesn't. He likes noodles at lunch, I don't. We don't insist on eating either of these meals together, though it can happen. Dinner is usually at seven and what we'll eat is agreed upon. I cook and he cleans up. Occasionally, it's the reverse. When there are guests, we both do both.

We have no rules about the division of labor, what's man's work or woman's, though physical strength puts chores like hauling propane tanks or wielding the chainsaw in Shingo's hands.

I do most of the grocery shopping - I can read English. And help spread gravel on the road.

He uses the chop saw and the longhandled axe to cut wood for the fires. I stack it in the woodpile, and cut up branches and bundle them for kindling. The time-consuming but satisfying work of cutting branches down to woodstove size he remembers as "grandfather's job," so I'm known as "o jii san," while I lop and chop.

I can change the water filter with ease, but if plumbing's needed, it's, "Over to you."

He does the laundry at the laundromat - it's heavy. I bake and make jam. Both of us can sew. Vacuuming happens when one of us spots a dust bunny, if there's enough electricity.

Being together 24 hours is something we're used to. We know we sometimes need to escape, that it's important to have time alone. If one wants to go to the beach and the other doesn't, nobody insists. If one wants to go to India and the other doesn't, that's okay, too. But, talking about it last night, we agreed that neither of us would want to live off the grid alone for very long. It's so much easier with two people working in tandem.

Having no rules calls for real respect for everything that gets done because under our system we could theoretically slack off indefinitely.

There's a lot of "Kansha shite imas," which means, "I appreciate you." There's: "Thanks for going to the dump." "Domo arrigato cleaning shower curtain." "Thanks for getting water." "Thank you make bed."

111

All this thanking, under other conditions, might be unnecessary, even boring, but here it spurs us on to all the waiting tasks.

There's also a lot of "I love you!" and, "I love you, too!" – go ahead, cover your ears, I don't blame you – but there's a similar amount of "I love this highway!" or "I love this fern!" expressed with equal emotion.

Rulelessness requires co-operation, too. If I want to go to the library and he wants to go to the hardware store but neither wants to go with the other, who gets the truck?

"Hey, Shingo! Rock, scissors, paper."

There are no rules for the weather. What happens one year doesn't happen the next. April on our windward side of The Big Island, we were told, was usually sunny with occasional showers. But not this year.

This year, 2006, record rain was causing damage and death. On Kauai Island, it had burst a reservoir, causing a tidal wave which wiped out houses down to their foundations and washed the inhabitants off a cliff and out to sea. Seven people died. On Ohau there were floods, and highway closures, and sewage overflow pollution problems.

We were getting only the tail ends of these terrible storms but they were keeping us damp and chilly, and mostly indoors, using lights and other electricity-eaters, making us totally dependant on that bane of our existance, the loudmouth generator. It was time to have a meeting and make some off-grid decisions.

We needed more power. But not from solar panels. To further enlarge the solar system, at great expense, would have diminishing returns at our place, which, even without the 100 year rains, was always going to be in a rainforest. Our next investment had to be in a top-of-the-line generator.

I started doing the research with some trepidation. I didn't want to make a mistake, though based on our adventures to date, that might be impossible.

The new generator should be as quiet as possible, easy to start, easy on gas, long wearing, large enough to meet our electrical needs but small enough for us to heft and handle.

Was there one which would come on automatically when we were low on power? Or one we could start from inside the house? Apparently so, but they were larger, noisier, and more expensive.

After carefully considering our options, we decided which one to buy and, calling around, found it in stock in Hilo. As planned, we'd pay for it by selling the mother-in-law kitchen and our leftover solar inverter – not that we had no money in the bank, but better to be frugal.

I put ads in the paper and the kitchen cabinets sold. But after two weeks we still had the stove, fridge, some louver doors, and the inverter.

"We have time," Shingo said. He was right: having waited so long, we could wait a little longer.

Meanwhile, one of his art dealers from L. A. came to visit for the day. She was staying in sunny Kailua Kona at a fancy resort. We'd stayed at the same resort for one night the previous November when someone gave us a gift certificate they couldn't use.

What luxury: all-day sun followed by the splendor of a sunset on the ocean, too much food, a king-sized bed, a deep bathtub with very hot running water and very thick towels, air conditioning, television and movies, but by morning it had all worn thin. There were too many rules.

Signs at the edge of the ocean, with its white sand beach, warned "No Swimming." If anyone was going to swim it must be at manmade pools and beaches within the hotel grounds: so safe, so perfectly groomed, provided with lifeguards, lounge chairs, dry beach towels on demand, and icy mai tais delivered to your side-table.

There were dolphins in a shallow pond, doing tricks for us tourists, a stone's throw from their home in the deeps of the Pacific. You could join them in jail, observe them, even pet them, as long as you were over 5 years old, signed a waiver for insurance purposes, and paid $199.00 per person for 20 minutes of "dolphin encounter."

Schools of mullet swam free in a river on the property where a sign said "No Fishing."

At a restaurant we were reminded, "No Shirt, No Shoes, No Service."

We longed for the dance of the wild dolphins at dangerous Kehena Beach where they spun and flipped for their own amusement. We wondered, where's the local kid, armed with a bamboo pole and bread on his hook, being taught by Dad or Mom to fish for mullet? Where's his older brother who's learning to use a net? We wanted to get home and hear Charlie Nihipali, shirtless and shoeless, mutter "Where you been?"

Even if, for us, it had offered nothing real, the hotel in sunny Kona was ideal for our guest, travelling with a small child, who, at our house, had to stay indoors because of rain and mud. That April, in the mountains of East Hawaii, we were getting a little too much reality from nature's lack of rules.

At The Merrie Monarch hula festival in Hilo, we ran into Shingo's old friend, that other city boy Yuki Oda, who was still living in L. A.

"It's so great here," I told him, only slightly over-selling. "We're living in paradise and it's all your fault."

He and his wife were enthusing about selling his house in Captain Cook, buying raw acreage, and creating a small community off the grid. Their eyes shone with anticipation, as had ours when we were considering the lifestyle.

"Before you dive in, you might want to come and visit, hear what we've been going thr. . . uhh, we've learned a few things about off-grid life in the short time we've been here," I said.

They came, but their plans had hit a snag. Land on the sunny side of the island was too expensive.

"Come to this side. Move up here," I suggested, as the rain, which had been non-stop all day, came plastering onto the roof, outshouting even the racket from the generator.

"Mmmm, maybe," said Yuki, perhaps his polite Japanese way of saying, "Are you out of your mind?"

At this writing, he hasn't sold his house in Captain Cook but hasn't moved there either. He continues to live, as his sister said he might, in The City Of The Angels.

There is one rule I try to observe: the one about living within our means. But the generator was giving too much trouble, taking too many hard pulls to start. Shingo complained of pain in his shoulder. And the noise, the incurable, unbearable noise was getting us down.

Should we replace the sparkplug, try to keep going? No! Enough! We were going to replace the generator whether the rest of the kitchen sold or not. We were going to buy a new one. "Today!"

The new generator cheered us up.

Now there's an understatement. From the first moment we turned it on, we knew it would change our lives.

As April ended, the mother-in-law refrigerator, range, louver doors and inverter got sold, but we'd spent more than expected on ads and gone way over on our phone minutes, so we hadn't quite covered the cost of our brand new generator. But we wouldn't have cared if we'd spent our last dime. That pricey little generator was worth its weight in diamonds. That perfect little generator was the paddle for our off the grid canoe.

12

MAY IN PARADISE
Da Paddle

Americans, and pre-Americans, living in a land of lakes and rivers, and their Canadian cousins, have traditionally used a slim canoe, and a sylphlike paddle with a slender blade, to glide silently over glassy surfaces or manoever in white-water, to twist and turn, back-paddle, or stroke for speed. Hawaiian paddles are giants by comparison, like the Polynesians themselves, with strong wide blades to move their heavy double-hulled canoes over vast blue-water oceans.

The paddle, high tech for the ancients, gets you where you want to go and acts as a rudder to keep you on course. It takes you face-first into your future, unlike an oar, which pulls you through the water backwards.

A paddle seems a fitting metaphor for our life-propelling new generator, even though it was made in Japan where an oar is customary.

What a machine! I want to write love letters to it. I want write songs about it. I want to hug it. I do pat and congratulate it every time I use it.

I'll compare its friendly color to a jolly red anthurium, its inky black trim to the night sky before the stars come out, its shiny gas cap to the full moon rising. I'll tell of its delightful fuel guage, so easy to read, its winsome knob which turns the gas on with a flick of the wrist, its artful choke which slides like silk, and its magical key which turns it on and off WITHOUT A PULLCORD!

This new generator is the key to our life off the grid, and its key is the key to the key. One twist of that subtle silver key and the generator begins to purr like the well-tuned engine it is, so quiet we can use it whenever we like.

We can use it in the early morning, we can use it late at night, we can use it anytime we need a volt.

It's fast, too. It makes electricity in half the time of our old clunker. So it doesn't guzzle gas: two gallons will run it for almost a week.

Shingo and I have just been swooning over it again and asking ourselves for the hundredth time why we waited so long to get it. Once again, we didn't know the difference.

But other island residents did. When I put an ad in the paper to sell the old generator, not one call came in. And notices on bulletin boards went unanswered. We finally gave the beast to Dave and when he turned it on for the first time I almost jumped out of my skin. That poor man: what he had to live with day and night for months. Thank heavens he hardly ever uses it.

By the middle of May we were making plenty of power, not only with the new generator, but with the sun, which was playing hide and seek again, coming out in the morning for an hour or two, then giving way to pouring rain, then sun, then rain, then sun, then rain.

I'd just get out to the Do It Yourself garden with lopping shears, then have to duck a shower. Or hang a towel on the backyard clothesline, then have to run and grab it. This latter scenario is known at our place as "the clothesline jinx" – hang anything on the line and it will surely rain.

Still it was nice to have some sun, a beam or two to call our own.

I tried again to grow vegetables in my makeshift greenhouse, this time putting seeds in pots rimmed with copper tape which, I was told, would repel slugs. As soon as I replanted, everything came up and the copper tape worked. No slug damage. Saucers of beer as slug bait also worked and I caught lots of them of every slimy size and color. I can now say with authority that Hawaiian slugs prefer Bud Light to Miller High Life.

I still had to worry about pigs breaking in. A friend suggested barbed wire and brought a partial roll, which he'd used to make a fence. Trying to lift the heavy roll and needing Shingo's strength to work with the springy stuff gave me new admiration for farmers and ranchers, the fence builders.

We strung two lines of it around the bottom of the enclosure where pigs might root or wander in, and after installing it there was no sign of them. But it had nothing to do with barbed wire, they'd just gone away. Like Fidel Castro who, they say, used to sleep in a different house every night, pigs are constantly on the move, fearing assassination.

With the new generator smoothing our way, we now wished we had a big propane tank – there's always that next thing to want. The obvious advantage to a big propane tank was that The Gas Company would fill it. It would also make a clothes-dryer possible. I started inquiring about it, and as usual had to overcome no address difficulties, but the Gas Company's estimator finally said she'd come by on a Tuesday.

She didn't, and when I called to ask why, she said she'd turned back. Her propane tankers could never come down Road Nine because of overhanging trees on the street and a sagging telephone wire at the corner, so why even bother with an estimate.

Calling the phone company to fix that part of the problem was a necessary, if unwanted, chore. I made several attempts to reach the service department but there'd been a change of ownership – one phone company swallowing another - causing who's-in-charge service difficulties and a traffic jam on the switchboard. When I heard a pre-recorded announcement that there'd be a 24 minute wait, I hung up and gave up, not having 24 minutes to spare on my mobile phone.

The Gas Company's estimator, after hand-wringing from me, took pity, and agreed to come and consult. She thought we probably could get a big propane tank, provided we could solve the tree and wire problems.

But as she eyed our existing propane delivery system, there was tongue-clucking and head shaking: "Copper tubing - no, no - not to code."

There were limited options about where the tank could go since her truck driver must be able to see it from the street: in other words an eyesore of a tank would have to be plopped in front of the house. She thought the ideal spot would be in front of Shingo's studio where it would dominate our entryway, a proposal that would have had Martha Stewart feeling faint: it couldn't exactly be hidden by a wreath.

We came to a compromise. The tank could be installed outside the mother-in-law suite, and screened by a hedge of gardenias.

But there was more: a filled tank, the first to be delivered, would cost $500.00 and need refilling several times a year, at around $350.00 a time, but first we'd need to have special galvanized pipe put in, leading from the tank's location to wherever we wanted to use a gas appliance.

At $15.00 per foot, plus labor, we knew we were looking at $3,000.00 minimum, but decided to get some real numbers from a plumber, who took more than a week to come and confirm our suspicions.

He also let us know, after crawling around under the house, that all our regular plumbing was 1/4 inch too small and the wrong type of PVC, and that our toilets weren't properly vented.

Thank you so much Mr. Off The Grid, Mr. I Did It Myself. You skimped again.

But since we weren't planning to drink the water, and the toilet vents just needed pipe added on, we couldn't get too incensed. Two more things would be added to the list of "when the time is right," things that got pushed further and further back behind "you need it for survival" items.

One of those items now made itself known. The quietness of the new generator pointed up the noisiness of the water pump. It was groaning and straining in short, breathless bursts, still sounding like a cane toad, but a terminally ill one.

I called Hilo Propane to talk about the pump, but couldn't understand what they were telling me. I ended the call, saying, "I guess I have to get the plumber, huh?" feeling frustrated, knowing he'd just been here, and it would, again, probably take a week to get him back.

A few minutes later, the manager of Hilo Propane, Bob DeFrancisco, having overheard only one side of the conversation, having obviously asked questions, and apparently being a direct descendant of Santa Claus, called me back.

"You don't need a plumber," he said, "You need Michael: he knows everything about on-demand hot water systems. Here's his number. He'll help you."

Am I wrong in thinking this went way beyond business as usual, or even small town kindness? I can tell you I was, and still am blown away by it. I'll never forget that generous phone call, which directed us to a man who totally saved our bacon.

"Well, for starters," said Michael McMillan of Michael's Repair, who came the next day, "there's no air in your pressure tank. Probably never did have any in there from what you're telling me."

"And," he said, reaching for his tools, suppressing a grin, "your pump's in backwards."

Mr. Grid The Off! Mr. Myself It Did I! First the backwards solar panels, now this?

"And your water heater's too small."

"Yeah. We know. We know."

I asked if he could recommend a hit man who specialized in dyslexic penny-pinching builders, but he just laughed. And so did we, once the repairs were made.

Try as we might, we couldn't stay "nose joint" at the man who built our paradise. So he didn't know enough about the technicalities – we don't either. So he always tried to save a penny – so do we. Just a glance at his first-rate landscaping, and all the other things he did well, and he had to be forgiven, even loved.

Though, once in a while, when the shower emits its meager stream of water, when it gets too hot or too cold, I admit I feel put out about that extra 1/4 inch of pipe, and the too-small hot water heater, and no galvanized delivery system for propane gas. At such moments, I send a five dollar Japanese epithet in the direction of Sarasota, Florida.

"Akab!" I hiss. That's "Baka!" backwards. I'll bet his ears are burning.

During this third semester of Off The Grid University, Shingo sold another painting and a print in L. A., and got well represented at The Fine Art Associates in Honolulu. He was offered an expense-paid group show in Los Angeles for June, and a solo show on Hawaii Island at Stephen Freedman's experimental *"idspace"* gallery for July. The sun can come out in more ways than one.

By late April the sun in the sky came out and stayed out, more or less. "Sunny with a few light showers," was how the weather service described it. This sweeping generalization, which is often made by the weather service, rarely applies to our neighborhood, but suddenly, it did.

We were making 29 volts with just the sun: a new, exciting, experience. I could vacuum or even bake without thinking too much about it. And the days were lengthening.

But don't worry, we still needed the generator at night. Electric rice cooker - our addiction, DVDs, computer at night, more lights: we were going back to old habits of conspicuous consumption. We were also conspicuously more comfortable.

Our daytime temperature rose to 79 degrees. We didn't need a fire at all. The house was drier and mold didn't cause our nostrils to twitch.

But in the heat the truck started to stink and we didn't know why. Did a mouse get in there and die? Did we run over a frog and have its guts rotting underneath? More likely it was something like shrimp juice from the groceries leaking onto the rug. Many cleaning products later we could drive the truck without holding our noses.

All that sun helped the vegetables to grow in my temporary greenhouse. It also caused the sheet-plastic roof to crack, then sag, then disintegrate, as before, in the next heavy rain, whacking the plants again.   On the scoreboard for growing vegetables it was Rainforest 100 – Canadian 0.

But hey, we had a brand new generator, our sturdy paddle, keeping us in smiles.

When telling Shingo's name to someone, I used to say, "It's Honda, like the car." But nowadays I always say, "It's Honda, like the generator."

13

JUNE IN PARADISE
Chickens

Shingo's a lover of cats and I'm a fan of dogs but we've decided we won't have either of them as pets. It's too muddy here.

In the grass, mud lurks under every blade, and in some low spots, when it's been raining, which is almost always, there's that mud that slurps around your rubber boots. When pigs come rooting, there's mud all over the place, and, the way things look, it's going to be that way, on and off, indefinitely.

This means a dog would rarely if ever be invited into the house. It would have to be chained outside or in a covered pen. A cat would have to be always an indoor cat or an outdoor one. Neither of us can limit the freedom of an animal that way. It would be better, we think, not to have them at all.

But Shingo was dying to raise chickens. Three of our friends had them in their yards, tottering around and clucking in their painterly feathers, providing a bounty of eggs.

He needn't have "boisterous" roosters, he learned, the eggs kept coming without them. As a bonus, the hens might eat coqui frogs and they'd devour bugs in our garden.

Sometimes, I knew, they had bugs of their own: bird mites, which will bite humans. Some people aren't bothered by bird mite bites. Some are allergic, like me.

The allergy was diagnosed years ago when I was working on *The Bob Newhart Show* and a bird built a nest in the office air conditioner.

I was covered in bites, not the mosquito pink-bump variety, which go away in a few days, but flaming red welts which spread into each other and itch, itch, itch, for weeks.

It happened again in Downtown when Shingo put a baby dove back in its nest and I held the ladder for him.

"Allergic to bird mite bites," might not be the best entry on a resume for co-chicken-farmer, but I wanted to apply for the position. Keeping chickens, collecting their eggs, but never killing them for the pot, fit my Mother Earth meets Madame Pele vision of a full, rich, Hawaiian country life.

In early June there was an opportunity to adopt a sitting hen from ceramic artist Clayton Amemiya. The hen was a jungle fowl, and they can fly, so they're perfect as free-range chickens. They wander around in the daytime, but they sleep in trees.

I thought their mites wouldn't be a problem since the birds would never be concentrated in one place. Just, during the time the babies were hatching, until they could fend for themselves, they'd all have to stay in a coop, where they could be protected.

Toward the end of June Shingo'd be leaving for three weeks for his group show in L. A. He was supposed to be painting furiously so he could exhibit new work. But fertilized eggs under a warm hen won't wait, so he needed to build a chicken coop.

He built the coop never having seen one and without much information: our chicken-owning friends weren't very specific. He had to keep the chicks safe from mongoose and rats and cats, and keep them dry and warm. And he had to feed and water them. Beyond that, the mother hen would take care of them, that was the message.

He decided to use a lean-to at the back of our garden for the coop, the former site of the woodpile. The original wood was all gone now, burned over the long wet winter and spring, and newly cut logs had been moved to a drier place under the house.

The lean-to already had a tarpaulin roof and back wall, and guava poles as supports. As protection from predators, Shingo put chicken wire over everything, including the floor of the structure. He built a chicken wire covered door, tightly fitted to its supports.

To be doubly safe, he made a wire-cloth covered interior roosting box for the mother and babies, with a guillotine door at one end. No doggone mongoose or rat or cat was going to sneak in and eat his baby chicks.

We went to Hilo to the feed supply and bought a watering device, a feed container, and chicken food. Shingo, who does nothing by halves, bought a 50 pound sack of feed. The cost was only $20.00, a reasonable price for the coming abundance of eggs.

With everything prepared, it was time to go and get the hen. But when we got to Clayton's he had two hens, one barn door red, one streaky beige, sitting on fifteen eggs. This might have been more chickens than we'd bargained for, but there was no way to separate them.

They were roosting placidly on Clayton's open porch in a sturdy wicker basket with a handle, so it was a simple matter to move them into a cardboard box for the trip to their new home.

When Clayton told us we'd probably start getting hatchlings right away, based on the gestation time for eggs, Shingo lit up like a child in anticipation.

When they grew up, I wondered, where would they lay their eggs? "Anywhere they want," he said, pointing out an egg nestled in some socks in a laundry basket and another on the seat of a chair.

On the way back to our house we decided the hens should have names. Coming from artist to artist we'd name them after artists. Women, of course. I was hoping one of them could be named after a writer and proposed Gertude Stein. But Shingo didn't know the name and couldn't pronounce "Gertrude." After all, they were his chickens, so one would be "Frieda" after Freida Kahlo and one would be "Georgia" after Georgia O'Keefe.

We worried about Frieda and Georgia as we got closer to home. We hoped they and their eggs wouldn't be too jarred and jolted on lumpy, bumpy Road Nine - it was time to haul gravel to fix the road again, we just hadn't gotten around to it.

Shingo drove suitably slowly and the hens hardly clucked from the back of the truck as we navigated our ride-'em-cowboy road. But whether they were traumatized or comfortable, we couldn't tell.

They didn't complain when Shingo carried them out of the truck and moved them down to the chicken coop. There was no fuss, either, when he removed their basket from the shipping box and slid them into the roost.

He filled the newly purchased chicken feeder and put it, and the watering device, in with them, talking in a soothing voice as he shut the guillotine door, backed away, and sidled out. Quietly closing the main door to the coop, he left them to themselves.

But neither of us could stay away. We had to keep visiting to make sure they were alright. Their home at Clayton's had been in a warmer, drier part of the island. Were they okay at our place? Was it too cold or damp for them? We hovered like new parents. Would they eat the food Shingo put out? Would they drink the water?

Clayton had said that sitting hens usually left their nests only once a day to eat and drink. On my second trip to the coop the food was already gone. Most of it had been eaten but the container was tipped over and there was a pile of food on the floor. I went to tell Shingo he ought to fasten the food-holder to the side of the roost so it wouldn't spill.

When he went to do that he found a big ball of chicken manure, the size of an egg, on the wooden floor of the roost. He thought he should have newspaper in there for easier cleanup. The best way to install it would be to remove the hens.

I heard a sudden cacaphony, furious clucking that shrieked, "Buzz off!" "Take a hike!" "Get lost!" and went to the coop to find Shingo being attacked by an angry red hen, though the beige one was sitting quite calmly on the eggs.

"She bite me!" he said, laughing and pointing. "That one Frieda! She so passion!" Now we knew who was who.

With the hens parked to one side, Shingo decided that rather than use newspapers he'd customize the floor of the roost. I heard a hammer flying as he created a slatted bottom for it with a removable subfloor. Chicken poop would fall between the slats and he could take it out on the tray.

I went to see his handiwork once the hens were back in the roost and worried out loud that when chicks were born they might fall through the slats in the floor. But it was getting towards sundown, time for Frieda and Georgia to be going to sleep. They'd had quite a day and so had we.

"Why American say 'chicken' meaning scared?" Shingo asked me as we were having dinner, though he seemed to want to answer the question himself. "Chicken not scared. Chicken is warrior, tough, Samurai mother," he said. "She mad, she bite me. She not scared."

"Uh, huh," I answered, knowing I'm a chicken in the American sense.

It's true, I am a chicken, a 'fraidy cat, a worry-wart. Fear is my middle name. It's made me quit when I was winning, start when I should have stopped, stay when I should have left. Right now, I'm scared our water pump is going to break again. It's coming on when nobody's running water.

That night I noticed a couple of itchy bites, but couldn't say it was from bird mites. Mosquitoes tended to congregate down by our old woodpile, and tiny spiders were everywhere. Wanting to be more of a Samurai chicken, I didn't tell Shingo about it, just slipped into the bathroom and slathered on the anti-itch cream.

Our first baby chick was born the next morning. Shingo made the discovery of a little ball of fluff in the basket. He ran, and I'm not exaggerating, to call me, "Honey-chan! You have to see!" And we both hurried down to see the newborn, "Peep, peep, peep," the cutest thing in the world.

In ecstasy, he called Clayton to announce the birth. "Everything fine!" he reported proudly. Now he could start painting.

But next time I went to peer, the chick had hopped out of the basket and was falling through the slats in the floor. "Shingo-o-o!"

With Frieda pecking and squalling, he slid newspaper over the slats to support the chick. But the chick was too small to hop back in the basket.

"How about a ramp?" I asked. He thought that might work, found a piece of plywood and, risking Frieda's wrath, laid it against the basket.

The chick, only hours old, knew instinctively how to take care of itself. It climbed up the ramp and jumped back in with its mother.

Chickens like me are afraid they can't or won't take care of themselves. Coming from a long line of Irish alchoholics it's not an unreasonable fear.

People I loved self-destructed. I'm scared it's in my genes. So far so good – I'm alive and kicking at the age of mumble mumble, but, you know, you'd like to be sure.

I wonder, sitting here thinking about it, whether moving off the grid, with all its demands, isn't one more way to prove to myself that I'm made of stronger stuff.

When Shingo's painting I try not to disturb him, but the next time I looked in on the coop, the red-feathered mother, Frieda, was using the ramp. With her weight on it, it was wobbling. Her fuzz-ball chick was underneath, threatened with doom.

I gave him the news, suggesting he make hooks for the ramp so it couldn't fall down and nobody'd be flattened like road-kill. This time he wore heavy gloves, knowing Frieda's temperament, and despite her outrage, managed to install the hooks - Shingo's not a guy who chickens out.

The thing I really chicken out about is running out of money. I'm probably not alone in this. But my net worth is about the same as it was fifteen years ago, and I haven't had what my mother would describe as "a real job" in all that time.

I know that money goes around and comes around, my mate is the poster boy for this, but I still can't help squeezing a nickel as hard or harder than Mr. Off The Grid, Mr. I Did It My Way, Mr. "Zowie, I Saved 42 Cents!"

I'm still squeezing them over the big propane tank. I haven't even hired the plumber.

That afternoon I noticed I was getting more bites, and these were definitely from bird mites.

You can tell a bird mite bite because of its location. They bite where anything's tight: the backs of your knees where they fold; in the creases under your arms; where there's elastic - your belt line, your bra line, your panty line. Not to be indelicate, but bird mites bite in places you'd rather not be scratching in public. You'd rather not be scratching there at all.

I told Shingo about it but wanted to Samurai on. That baby chick was pretty terrific.

But by nightfall I could count about eight bites and they were all welting up. I showered and put cream and spray on them and took an ibuprofen caplet but they were no-sleep itchy. Three times in the night I was up, doctoring them.

By mid-morning, more than fifteen bites were showing, and they were so uncomfortable I had to make a hard decision.

I showed them to Shingo and dejectedly told him I didn't think I could take care of the chickens while he was in Los Angeles. The birds were all in one place and their mites were, too. By the time he returned after three weeks in California, I'd be one big red welt.

He agreed it wasn't going to work and called Clayton to say we needed to bring back our guests. Three days, two nights, they'd been with us, like a Kona vacation package: checkout time is noon.

Clayton sympathised and said he had someone else who'd take them. Now Shingo had to get them out of the coop and into a box. He told me to stay far away.

But Frieda's screeching was enough to raise hair on a Zen monk. I had to go and see what was happening.

"CLUCK CLUCK CLUCK CLUCK CLUCK!!! BACAWWWW!!! CLUCK! CLUCK! CLUCK! BACAAWWWW!!!" Frieda was flying at Shingo, like a fighting cock on the attack. Even the docile Georgia pecked viciously at him. He managed, under extreme abuse, to put their basket with the eggs and the baby into the box, but they had no intention of going in. He finally scooped Frieda in as she flew at him, then picked up Georgia by the neck and tossed her in.

I followed him to the truck and opened the tailgate so he could load and leave, feeling guilty for causing him so much trouble and spoiling all his fun.

After he left, I took the sheets off the bed, sprayed bug spray everywhere, took a shower, changed clothes, and put everything which might have been exposed to mites in a quarantine pile on the back porch. When Shingo returned, he took the pile to the laundromat to wash it.

Awww, Shingo. His delight in Frieda and Georgia and the baby chick was so endearing. His anticipation of more little fluff balls had him glowing. My allergy had ruined everything.

When he came back from the laundromat, I met him at the door with a long face and started to apologize, but he stopped me.

He lowered his jeans, then his jockey shorts. He was covered in mite bites, too.

"Shikatanai," we comforted each other, "Cannot be helped," as we went into the bathroom for anti-itch cream and spray.

I'm afraid of failure, even though I know that failure can be the best, the kindliest, teacher. It'll show you where your faults lie. It'll show you who your friends are. You'll find out, happily, who loves you despite your flaws. At least that's been my experience. And yet, I'm still afraid of failure.

I'm no longer afraid, however, of the failure of our water pump.

I just figured out that it was turning on for a garden hose not completely turned off. Since I turned the hose off, the pump is properly humming, and so am I: that Rocky theme again. Perhaps, in this frame of mind, I should pick up the cellphone and call the plumber about that big ugly propane tank.

My "boisterous," "ambivalent," "frugal," girlfriend, in Beverly Hills, is known to her intimates as The Queen Of Returns.

If she gets it home from the store and doesn't like the fit, she returns it. If she doesn't like the buttons she returns it. If she finds out it's gone on sale, she returns it, and buys it again at the lower price.

When I call her - always for free on a Saturday - I don't say "Hello," I ask, "What are you returning?"

On the first Saturday in June she returned a hair product because it was drying her hair. Not one bottle, twenty bottles. She returned a five-year supply.

On the third Saturday in June I called her to say that, despite the daring hair goop return, her position as Queen had been usurped. Never in her lifetime will she be able to say that she returned chickens.

I am a chicken. I have no guts. No guts no glory, they say. But here, off the grid, in a rainforest in Hawaii, it doesn't matter whether I have guts or not. The glory is ongoing. It's just a matter of whether I'm willing to put up with it.

14

JULY IN PARADISE
Home At Last

What is "home"?

A long e-mail from Downtown friends who've travelled the world and settled in Turkey says they haven't found it. They're moving to a remote island in Thailand.

Another old neighbor in a temple-dominated Hindu town in India, where he lives like a barefoot king, says he has; and so have our Downtown chums studying and performing contemporary mime in Paris.

Each one's choice of a place to call home is so different. And each one's chosen home is a world away from where they were born.

The two in Turkey are from England and Vietnam. The pair in Paris are from Korea and Brazil. Our friend in India, an American, was born in Zimbabwe.

And we two, from Canada and Japan? We're still somewhat astonished to find ourselves living off the grid in a Hawaiian mountain rainforest.

But we're not "pioneers" as some off-grid websites describe the lifestyle. Just two dummies trying to learn how to use both old and new technologies to make ourselves comfortable in a dramatic environment.

Our grandparents, who lived with wood or kereosene or charcoal stoves, and ice-boxes, and handpumps, and oil lamps, and outhouses, and horses, and wagons, and unpaved roads; no central heating, hand-crank phones if they had them, no computers, and certainly no internet, would laugh at our "softies" idea of a comfortable home, as would the early Hawaiians who lived quite comfortably with none of the above.

And so would the millions of people in "developing" countries who've never experienced "the grid"; like the bride, in rural Nepal, whom Shingo encountered as she and all her belongings were carried over a mountain by the men of a far-away village. There she'd meet, for the first time, and marry, the groom her parents had chosen for her, and there she'd make her new home.

Her house would be built of stones with a slate roof. The interior walls and floor would be made of a mixture of mud and dung. She'd cook over a spare wood fire in a shallow depression in the floor of the main room, sitting on a woven reed cushion. She'd serve and dine where she cooked, around the fire, using plates and bowls made of cleverly folded, easily disposable, leaves. She'd scrub her pots and cooking utensils with ash from the fire, and rinse them in water piped, using gravity flow, from a nearby stream to a tap in the center of the family compound, where she'd also do her laundry. After dark, her lighting would come from a kerosene lantern. Her bathroom would be a simple outdoor shelter of banana leaves and bamboo, with a hole in the ground and a pail of water for washing up.

Her new home, to the eye of an insider, would be a wealthy one, and to an outsider, simple and beautiful. But whether she dreamed of more modern conveniences or city life in Kathmandu, we'll never know.

What is "home"?

It's not just a roof over rooms. It's not just dinner on the table. It's not just being with someone you can laugh and cry with, or having family or friends or neighbors around and the mutual caring and giving that happens. It's not just having the freedom to create something of your own – a painting? a garden? a baby? - or even the soul-restoring aspect of a place. There's something more to it. An attitude. Gratitude?

Shingo left for his L. A. art exhibition in late June, planning to stay for three weeks. Before he left he put in a good supply of propane and drinking water and generator gas so I wouldn't have to think about it. I stayed in Hawaii to write, and itch and scratch.

The mites weren't gone. At the beginning of July, I was still being bitten.

I went to the library, downloaded mite information, and learned that mites could live for as long as a month without a blood meal. They could hide in cracks and crevices, in clothes or carpets, and wait until a warm body showed up.

But were they living on me? Were they living in my clothes? Were they living in the rug? Usually they lived on a chicken. But chickens don't take hot baths and chickens don't go to the laundromat. Chickens don't vacuum. Chickens don't iron, but then, neither do I.

While Shingo was gone, I wanted to use every possible moment to write. With the new generator, most marvelous tool, I could start early and end late. Every trip outside the house, for mail, for the internet, for garbage dumping, for grocery shopping, felt like an imposition. I kept putting off going to the laundromat, though that made no sense.

Making tea at the kitchen range, I told myself to just get on with it, go to the laundromat, and expose anything suspected of mites to the heat of a dryer. I didn't even have to wash everything. High heat would kill any mite.

Then, with a downward glance, I saw the oven. Just a second - no need to leave. Bake! Why not bake my clothes?

Loving the lunacy of it, I loaded clothes, a few at a time, onto cookie sheets, and baked them at 230 degrees for 45 minutes per suspected infestation.

Of course I had to use the generator, but that was now enjoyable. I could keep working. Nothing got scorched. And that was the end of the mites.

Being a chicken, I worried that Shingo might not be happy to come back to Hawaii. He was Downtown with all our remaining friends and the old party atmosphere. After the art show, they were going to Mexico, then camping in Joshua Tree desert, one of his favorite spots.

Before he left he'd told me, "I no want go. Many projects waiting me." They still were.

Even with our no-pressure rule, the list was daunting. Soon after he came back he'd need to go for propane, check the water level in the batteries for the solar system, and give the new generator its first oil change.

An ohia tree which fell over in the forest needed to be cut up for firewood, and a dead one threatening his studio had to be cut down.

And while he had the chain saw out, the overhanging branches on Road Nine needed attention. The roof gutters needed a clean-out. And it was long past time to put gravel on the road.

Did he really want to be a multiple-hyphenate: artist – gofer - mechanic – road repairman - forester - gutter guy?

Cellphone to cellphone communication was free. I could call, anytime, to Shingo "across the street" to share in the good news about his art exhibit, the paintings that had been sold, and say "Hi" to the friends he was seeing.

Youn Woo Chaa, at whose loft he was staying, told me, "Shingo's so changed. He has no edge to him. He's more like a country boy." But whether he thought so himself, I'd have to wait and see.

At the airport, his smile said it all: no "ambivalence" there.

"I home," he enthused, inhaling a big gulp of sweet Hilo air. He kept repeating it for days.

Whenever he's gone, I tell myself I'm glad to have time alone, time to write uninterrupted, eat steak which he doesn't like, watch British movies on DVD with complicated plots set in the 16th century, make a big mess and not clean up until I have to, do crossword puzzles and cryptograms with no music in the background, read The Economist from cover to cover in one sitting, garden long past dinner time. Now he was home. And one beatific smile from him let me know what bald-faced lies I'm capable of telling myself.

Shingo was outside singing off-key more lustily than usual. When I went to find out why, he explained that he'd had a good adventure while chainsawing the largest overhanging tree limb on Road Nine.

The limb, as it fell, hit his ladder, knocking him off. He threw the running chainsaw in one direction and tried to fall in another, but the ladder fell on his head. He was telling me, while laughing, that he almost lost his life or a limb of his own.

I heard him singing again when I came back, shuddering, into the house. It was something in Japanese, but though I couldn't understand one word, it sounded a lot like the theme from Rocky.

He cut down the dead tree near his studio, yelling "Timber!" a word I didn't know he knew. By now he did know how to cut the tree so it fell in the right direction, not on him, not on the roof.

He chain-sawed it, and the other fallen ohia, into pieces suitable for splitting, carried and stacked them under the house to dry.

He checked the solar-system batteries using an unfamiliar hydrometer, and spent a morning cleaning out the gutters.

For two days, he, neighbors Charlie and Felix, and I spread gravel on the road and our driveway, which Auntie Jean down the street, with whom we shared the cost, had ordered.

As he dragged himself into the house one evening, after days and days of hard physical labor, I'd never seen him so satisfied. He fell on the sofa, exclaiming, "Almost dead!" I knew he meant, "Completely alive!"

I thought, "I've dragged Shingo into my dream." But, I heard him sigh, from his prone position on the sofa, "The dream in the dream," which means it's 1000% his own.

Shingo had his first solo show on The Big Island, on the third weekend in July, at Stephen Freedman's private art gallery, in a tropical garden setting where every blooming plant was a shameless hussy.

For the afternoon opening, contemporary dancer Shizuno Nasu, elegantly costumed, thrilled the audience as she performed on an immaculate patch of lawn framed by rare palms and exotic flowers, blending elements of ritual Japanese movement with classical European music played on a cello.

In the background were two large hens and an enormous dog, all disregarding the goings-on.

Those chickens and that old dog, and Stephen Freedman's pretty nine year old daughter, Bella, wearing a fuzzy pale-blue knitted hat to match her dress, and very adult dangly earrings, but no shoes, tucked the event into a paradigm of place: a place without too many rules, without too many opinions, a wildly creative place, already a paradise, which, for me, now deserved a capital "P."

The rest of July opened its arms to us.

There was warm sunny weather with just enough rain at night to keep the garden healthy.

There was a sundown coqui frog hunt with neighbors from Road Eleven, during which we hand-caught six frogs but not the three at our place, which eluded even the pros. Shingo caught the one in Auntie Jean's banana tree that had been keeping her awake.

There was a trip to Black Sand Beach where a local kid climbed a fifty foot coconut tree with a knife in his teeth, picked green coconuts, slid back down, and opened one for us, so we could try the spoon meat.

There was a visit from the director of the Maui Arts & Cultural Center to see more of Shingo's work.

There was Obon Festival dancing on a Saturday night in the parking lot of Taishoji Temple, with world-class taiko drumming, and what looked like half the teenagers of Hilo, together with their younger siblings, parents, and grandparents, never sitting out a chance to dance the traditional steps in honor of their ancestors.

The next day, Sunday, at dusk, Shingo helped Reverend Akita officiate a moving ceremony on the banks of the Wailoa River, where we floated lanterns with messages dedicated to family members who had passed away. We followed one for Shingo's brother down the river to the sea.

Okay, it's true that the gravel Auntie Jean ordered for Road Nine was too small and sank into the potholes right away, but it worked really well on our driveway.

And, yes, the cover for our catchment tank ripped and fell into the water supply and Shingo had to spend hours up to his armpits in chilly water - "Don't pee!" - while we installed the new top.

But these were minor educational events, considering the breadth and height of our year-long learning curve.

On August 1st, we celebrated our first year off the grid with a home-made ceremony, going around and formally thanking Madame Pele on whose firey volcanic island we live; every bird, bug, rock, tree and plant we share it with; frogs, toads, pigs, chameleons; each room in the house; the old and new generators; all our off-grid equipment; Mr. I Did It My Way And I'm Glad, and even the solar contractor - now that we had a paddle of a generator, we could cut him some slack.

We thanked the earth and the heavens, the whacky weather, old friends, new friends, and all the gentle people of Hawaii Island for supporting our life, agreeing that we wouldn't mind living here forever.

Of course we can't. No question about it, we have to die. As our Zen friend, Paul Pang, wisely says, "Everyone is standing in line for it."

But we're not in a hurry to go first. There's just too much to do.

I need to plant vegetables again, but this time with in-depth research so my methods will be more compatible with Puna.

Shingo needs to fix the chainsaw, but first he has to find out how.

I have to add beneficial microbes to the cesspool, and it wouldn't hurt to wash the windows.

We have to go and swim in that monster wave at Kehena Beach and hope it doesn't drag us off to Fiji.

And snorkel with clouds of butterfly-fish at the marine refuge in Kapoho.

I have to trim the hapu'u fern trees, add a few hundred more orchids to their trunks, pick the bananas off our own tree which are actually ripening, think of ways to use up forty bananas all ripening at the same time, and finish this book.

Shingo has to paint, paint, paint. He has a show coming up at The Contemporary Museum in Honolulu.

We have to decide whether and when and what color to paint, paint, paint the house.

And get busy on the woodpile, and tromp down the pig damage, and take the truck for a tuneup, and do something about the multiplying coqui frogs, and get ready for more guests.

And I have to, I want to, I'm going to, I will call the plumber about that ugly-beautiful propane tank.

We've stopped blaming that other city boy, Yuki Oda, for our decision to move here. These days, we blame each other. When the late afternoon sun turns our jungly backyard into a golden-green photographer's fantasy; or when the full moon, as bright as a streetlight, casts our spindly shadows as we wander outdoors at night; or when dewdrops glitter on a spider-web early in the morning, we turn to each other and accuse: "This is all your fault!"

Seeing a new-born hapu'u frond, as yet unfurled, shaking its hairy fist in the fern power-salute; hearing Melodious Laughing Thrush sing a duet with his lover in the woods; eating one more mango, we're in Paradise.

Rubber boots and rainbows, our love/hate relationship with pigs, the turn of the key to the generator, Charlie Nihipali's stories, Felix's happy tiki, signs that say "SMILE," the smell of white ginger: we're home.

ACKNOWLEDGEMENTS
Thanks!

Slip-streaming the content of this book, when it came time to publish *OFF THE GRID WITHOUT A PADDLE* I decided to Do It Myself, through Lulu.com. The reasons were several:

It can take a couple of years for a publisher to put out a book. I thought it would be better to get it to you sooner, while the events in it are still fresh, and Lulu.com can do it in a flash.

Also, the book is printed to order – you order it from Lulu or Amazon or your local bookstore and they send one. One book! Just for the person, anywhere in the world, who wants it. Isn't that amazing? That means there are no leftovers, and you can have one now, or in a year, or whenever – it won't go "out of print."

Via Lulu, there's also an e-book.

So thanks to Lulu.com for making *OFF THE GRID WITHOUT A PADDLE* not only a reality, but widely available.

I want to thank Patti Millington, who lives nearby, for the design of the cover. She could write her own book about moving to the boonies. You can see more of her graphic art on the internet at HI Art Magazine, which she designs, and also her fine art: just Google her.

I very much thank Martin Rowe of Lantern Books, who read an early presentation of *OFF THE GRID WITHOUT A PADDLE*, for his enthusiastic advice and encouragement. And literary agent Mary Ann Naples of The Creative Culture, Inc. for her correspondence and professional opinion that this book would be successful because of word-of-mouth, not extensive publicity.

They, Shingo Honda, and I, and almost everyone mentioned by name in *OFF THE GRID WITHOUT A PADDLE* can be Googled, if you'd like to find out more about their pursuits. Many, including Shingo, have their own websites.

For Cita, who wrote and sang about us moving "across the street" see "Cita Y Sus Munecas Rotas," and for her "boyfriend-for-life, guitarist from heaven" see "Ricardo Ochoa: After Avandaro, the black hole of Mexican rock."

ACKNOWLEDGEMENTS

For Suzi Gillette, our "real estate angel" see "Suzi's Hawaii Realty & Travel." Like us, she fell in love with The Big Island, bought a house here, and now knows the island like the back of her hand.

For Michael McMillan of Michael's Repair, who's rescued us more than once since that first time - he even talked us through an electrical crisis on the 4th of July when we had a houseful of guests - just Google. He's also in the Hawaii Telephone Directory if you need his services (in East Hawaii only) when your propane fridge, or hot water heater, or solar system breaks down.

Any product or company or catalogue I've named can be found on the internet. I've only named those I can recommend without reservation, feel grateful for having discovered, and therefore thank.

I also want to thank Rich Reha, who's not mentioned in the book because we didn't meet him until our second year off the grid. He's an electrical engineer, who, out of the kindness of his heart, gave us a tutorial about our solar system, then installed what we call "Rich's switch," a handy switch beside our bed which we can use to turn off our under-the-house invertor at night, and save enough electricity for toast in the morning!

Most of all, my thanks to you, for taking your valuable time to read *OFF THE GRID WITHOUT A PADDLE.* I hope you got a laugh or two and maybe some useful information.

If it's your dream to live off the grid, I hope nothing I've said will dissuade you. Anything that went wrong for us has been more than offset by how much we've learned from living on The Big Island with the wonderful people who belong to it. The proof is that we're still here and loving every minute.

Depending on your level of interest, and on what happens next in our gridless environment, there may be more stories to come.

Thanks everyone!

Made in the USA
Lexington, KY
25 August 2010